BUILDING KING'S

BELOVED COMMUNITY

BUILDING KING'S
BELOVED COMMUNITY

Foundations for Pastoral Care

and Counseling with the Oppressed

D O N A L D   M .   C H I N U L A

WIPF & STOCK · Eugene, Oregon

Wipf and Stock Publishers
199 W 8th Ave, Suite 3
Eugene, OR 97401

Building King's Beloved Community
Foundations for Pastoral Care and Counseling with the Oppressed
By Chinula, Donald M.
Copyright©1997 Pilgrim Press
ISBN 13: 978-1-60899-143-3
Publication date 10/1/2009
Previously published by United Church Press, 1997

I dedicate this book to my mother, Mrs. Mairess Mhango Chinula, who must often wonder if the sufficiency and abundance of God's grace includes her as well. Her quiet strength, indomitable spirit, and simple virtue have inspired my labors.

I acknowledge with gratitude the grant awarded me by Stillman College's Mellon Endowment Project for Faculty and Curriculum Development, funded by the Andrew W. Mellon Foundation, Inc., which enabled me to spend the summer of 1996 at the Martin Luther King Jr. Special Collections Department of Mugar Memorial Library, Boston University, to complete my research for this book. Dr. Howard B. Gotlieb and Mr. Charles Niles of that department were especially kind and helpful to me.

CONTENTS

FOREWORD

As I read and reflected on this book, I had poignant flashbacks from a pivotal day in my life. In retrospect, I recognize that the day was an unexpected turning point in my life journey, an experience of personal and professional transformation. That was the day I marched into Montgomery, Alabama, with thousands of others, following a prophetic hero, Martin Luther King Jr. I had been selected by my faculty colleagues to represent them because they knew that I had been captivated by King's vision of the beloved community. As I relive that decisive day, I can feel the flickering sparks of hope fanned as the moving column of thousands sang the rallying song of the civil rights movement, "We Shall Overcome." This was repeated again and again during the final miles of the protest march from Selma. I can remember the cloud of anxiety that also hung in my mind as I pictured Eugene "Bull" Conners with his fire hoses and police dogs, and realized that the lines of riot-ready soldiers were protecting us from the raw rage of some who shouted racist taunts from behind their crowd control lines.

Eventually we sat down in the wide street in front of the state capitol building. The Confederate flag on its dome fluttered in the hot, humid breeze as King challenged us with inspiring words of longing and hope that all oppressed people someday would be "free at last." Welcome relief from the thirst and anxiety that parched my throat came as a five-gallon jug filled with warm tap water was passed up and down the rows of listening marchers. The jug probably had been filled by thoughtful folks at the little black Baptist church nearby in the capitol plaza, a congregation that King had pastored years before. As I listened to his passionate plea for freedom and justice, I knew that drinking from that common cup—a jug of tap water—was the most powerful communion experience of my life. I also knew then that I could never again teach or practice pastoral care and counseling in ways that ignore the injustices and violence that are among the societal causes of most personal and family problems. I suspect that many others among the marchers also had experiences of inner confrontation, challenge, and change that day.

I have begun with this personal account to let you know why I'm particularly pleased that Don Chinula has written this significant book and why I hope you'll apply its insights in your ministry of care and counseling. In these pages you'll find a carefully researched overview of many of King's key ideas—concepts that challenge all privatized approaches to pastoral care, counseling, and ministry. You'll see how these approaches reflect the middle-class, white, male, Western origins of the modern pastoral care and counseling movement. And you'll find cogent evidence that all hyperindividualistic, privatized models are largely irrelevant to the life struggles and pain of the vast majority of the human family who are deeply wounded by injustice, violence, poverty, and social oppression.

Of course you may not want to read this book—if you really feel comfortable doing pastoral caregiving using cognitive maps from traditional individualistic approaches. But if you have even a tad of need to stretch your horizons of healing and enlarge your circles of caring, this book is for you. It will enable you to understand more fully why pastoral care and counseling of individuals and families, as important as these often are, are incomplete and short lived in their healing effects unless they include caring *for* and *through* social systems in transforming ways. The problem is that pathogenic institutional structures hurt persons on a wholesale scale while clergy and other counselors, teachers and therapists struggle to help them find healing and wholeness on an individual scale. In our society, overloaded as it is with injustice and violence, individualistic strategies clearly are not adequate. From both sociological and theological-biblical perspectives, nonsystemic counseling and therapy can be seen as middle-class luxuries that have diminished effectiveness when used beyond their limited circles of origin.

In the pages of this book, the author offers an alternative paradigm. He explores succinctly but with great clarity the pastoral care implications and applications of King's theologically and sociopsychologically grounded understanding of racism, classism, violence, and poverty. Dr. Chinula also sheds light on the dynamics of some parallel problems, including the "de-selfing" (or split-selfing) of women in our sexist culture and the "deculturalization" by which victims of colonialism are deprived of their indigenous cultural resources and wisdom. He uses King's thought to show how these institutionalized forces of "social leprosy" shatter individual and group self-esteem and demolish a unified, unifying sense of individual and group identity. Building on a foundation of these understandings, the author offers ways of enabling people so afflicted to move from disempowerment to empowerment in both their own wounded lives and their important groups. In short, the author applies King's brilliant insights to the basic healing–growth-facilitating process of enabling individuals and communities to move from what he called "nobodiness" to an affirmation of their God-given "somebodiness."

King's persistent pastoral-prophetic passion was to help bring God's healing power to the shriveled self-esteem, fractured identity, and feelings of ontological nothingness suffered by wounded victims of racial, ethnic, economic, and social oppression. This overarching motif in King's life and thought is explored in illuminating depth by Chinula. The resulting understandings are then applied to the theory and practice of pastoral caregiving. The author focuses on three crucial questions as he shows how pastoral caregiving is shaped by King's thought. Finding convincing answers to each of these questions is also relevant to the paradigm revisioning process that is needed to make caregiving and counseling more relevant to the changing world to which pastoral care and counseling will be called to respond in the next century.

The first question: What are the explicit norms that guide an empowering model of caregiving? Chinula's conclusion is derived directly from King's conviction that all persons, certainly including the poor, the oppressed, and the unlovable, must be respected for theological reasons. They must be given healing respect and loving care because God loves them and because each is made in the divine image. Another norm derived from King's sociotheological understanding and applied to caregiving is that the healing to wholeness process is essentially communal in both it setting and its methodologies. The author highlights King's awareness that these two norms are ideological twins both theologically and psychologically. As he puts it, "My somebodiness derives from God and thrives on your somebodiness."

The second paradigm-shaping question? What is an explicit evocative symbol to guide and empower such a model of caregiving? The empowering symbol is King's vision of the justice-based, wholeness-oriented community that he called the beloved community. This is the healing, empowering, nurturing environment of caregiving—a setting that is indispensable for effective caregiving with oppressed people. The third question: What are the essential tasks of caregiving, based on this explicit symbol and these norms? The author explores these four tasks as essential to the healing–growth-facilitating process—reclamation, conciliation, transformation, and transcendence.

This book has many strengths, some explicit and obvious, others implicit and hidden. If you have had your fill of superficial pop psychologizing and theologizing, you'll find it refreshing to read a volume that shows the solid results of the intellectual discipline of rigorous, doctoral research and yet is anything but pedantic and boringly bookish in its style. Another explicit strength is the author's grasp of pivotal ideas of many of the leading theological and psychological theory builders in our day, as their thought relates to King's insights. Chinula draws on numerous "underside psychologists," including feminists such as Anne Wilson Schaef and thinkers such as Paulo Freire and W. E. B. DuBois.

Thus he enhances the meaningfulness of King's key concepts as he applies these in developing an innovative paradigm for pastoral caregiving and counseling with the oppressed. Another obvious strength of this book for those of us who enjoy exploring the interface of theology and the human sciences is its applications of King's sociotheological awareness of the intimate, ontological heart and interrelatedness of the dynamics of powerlessness versus empowerment, of self-hatred versus genuine self-esteem, of fragmented versus unified self-identity. Life often teaches us lessons that we would rather not learn. The value of these lessons is usually evident only in retrospect. From my knowledge of Dr. Chinula's background, I am aware of an important implicit strength that enhances this book in important ways. I refer to the author's firsthand experiences of racism, classism, colonialism, and poverty. All of these help keep his approach grounded in the wounded and wounding world to which his paradigm is relevant. To be more explicit, it is clear that valuable learnings were derived from having grown up in a poor village of Malawi, where he experienced the esteem-damaging impact of colonialism; being expelled from high school for opposing oppression; living as a graduate student in the southern United States, followed by directing a program for disadvantaged black, Hispanic, and Native American youth; and then, before moving into graduate education in pastoral psychology and counseling, training and practicing as an attorney specializing in services for the economically and socially oppressed in Georgia and Arkansas.

It is obvious that for Chinula the social causes of personal problems are far more than simply complex theoretical issues calling for deeper understanding. The author has acquired both head wisdom and heart wisdom from his painful experiences of the social leprosy of oppressive institutional forces. There is no doubt that he has found deep meaning in his own life in the book's central motif—King's vision of the beloved community. That vision, as he says, "has fed my deepest hunger." Yet, it is important to note that this personal passion has not diminished his wrestling with tough-minded objectivity as he explores the dynamics of disempowerment, racism, sexism, and the grinding poverty that is inseparably linked with its conjoined twin—extreme wealth among powerful persons and nations.

Let me extrapolate from the book's main focus on care for and counseling of the disempowered. In my counseling and teaching experiences, on numerous occasions, I have found that a systemic, wholeness-oriented model of the healing–growth-facilitating process, aimed at healing and empowering people for reaching out to others, is effective with many persons who are not victims of major oppressions. A model comparable to the one developed in this book has liberating relevance for ministering to and with some who are the up-and-out as well as those on the underside of our society. It is surprising to discover that even occasional privileged, power-wielding oppressed-oppressors have a hidden longing to examine the ways they are subtly oppressed, the ways they suffer as well as profit from the "poverty of affluence." This is not to suggest that their oppression is in the same league as that of the obviously and profoundly oppressed, but only that a caregiving model with a prophetic dimension is useful in challenging them to examine the price they pay and society pays, wellness-wise, for their exploitative, privileged position.

On a personal level, I must say that reading this book has reminded me yet again that we who have the privilege of teaching others are among the most fortunate people in the world. It does my soul good to learn from a former graduate student. Thank you, Don Chinula, for making me more aware of the wisdom of one of my longtime heros, and for showing the healing, liberating, empowering potentials in that wisdom for our field!

What is my hope for you, the reader? In our turbulent, troubled society, torn apart by violence and injustices on many sides, may your understanding of the social causes of individual problems be deepened and broadened by reading this book. May its ideas help you move into the new century and millennium with a more empowering and liberating vision of pastoral caregiving. May its prophetic pastoral vision energize your ministry with those who know they are oppressed, but also with those not yet aware of their hidden need to help liberate themselves and others from the health-damaging forces in our social and natural environment.

HOWARD CLINEBELL
Professor Emeritus of Pastoral Psychology and Counseling
Claremont School of Theology

INTRODUCTION

Nobody is a nobody. Everybody is a somebody. Somebodiness is never earned or conferred. It is innate. It is a right. It is divine. It is ontological. My somebodiness derives from God and thrives on your somebodiness. The two are interdependent and mutually inclusive. My nobodiness disparages and degrades your somebodiness. You cannot rightfully claim to be somebody when you cause or tolerate my nobodiness.

This book is about community caregiving. It offers a paradigm for caregiving among the oppressed of any community. It approaches its task by studying and uncovering the keen psychological and theological insights Martin Luther King Jr. employed in presenting his message and program to the American public. These insights have such a significant bearing on the vocation of pastoral caregiving as to reshape and stretch it.

Specifically, the book discusses the significance of King's thought and life for the pastoral care and counseling of persons from oppressed groups or communities who present identity and self-esteem problems. It examines those aspects of King's thought and work that possess discernible elements of pastoral psychology and practical theology applicable to the pastoral care and counseling of such persons. It locates the practice of pastoral caregiving within the community of the afflicted, away from the rarefied offices of the caregiver. It offers a fresh way of understanding the root cause of identity crises and a feeling of worthlessness among the oppressed. It proposes a novel way of assessing and eradicating these emotional and spiritual perplexities.

By the time of his assassination on April 4, 1968, King had left a trail of stellar achievements and credits. Born in Atlanta, Georgia, on January 15, 1929, he entered Morehouse College at the tender age of 15 without first graduating from high school; a college entrance examination, which he had passed, made this transition possible.[1] Before completing his baccalaureate degree, King was licensed to preach and assist his father at the Ebenezer Baptist Church pastorate at the age of 18; a year later he was ordained to the Baptist ministry. King was graduated from Morehouse College in 1948, at the age of 19, and entered Crozer Theological Seminary that fall in order to pursue graduate study in religion.[2]

In 1951, King was graduated from Crozer as valedictorian with a B.D. degree, and entered Boston University School of Theology to seek the doctorate in systematic theology. He completed the Ph.D. degree in June of 1955 at the age of 26. While at Boston, King met Coretta Scott and the two were married on June 18,

1953. He was installed as pastor of the Dexter Avenue Baptist Church in Montgomery, Alabama, on October 31, 1954, at the young age of 25.[3] Thereafter his stature took a meteoric rise.

On December 5, 1955, King was unanimously elected president of the Montgomery Improvement Association (MIA).[4] The purpose of this organization was to respond in an organized but nonviolent manner to Montgomery's abuse of its black bus passengers. This abuse had been symbolized by the recent arrest of Mrs. Rosa Parks, a tired black seamstress, who refused to yield her seat on the bus to a white male. A total bus boycott, which lasted 381 days, was MIA's measured response.[5]

The violent response to the MIA's action directed at King and his family by Montgomery's white leadership catapulted King and the nascent civil rights movement onto the national and international scene. As death threats against him and his family increased, so also did King's resolve to change the human and social arrangements in Montgomery. On February 2, 1956, King caused to be filed a federal lawsuit to outlaw the city's travel segregation codes. The Supreme Court of the United States ruled in his favor on November 13, 1956, declaring all such local and Alabama state laws unconstitutional.[6] This ruling integrated all Montgomery buses and set the embryonic civil rights movement aflame.

The national and international media did not fail to take notice of this accomplishment. *Time* magazine featured King on the front cover of its February 18, 1957, issue. King and his associates met with the vice president of the United States, Richard M. Nixon, on June 13, 1957, and later on with President Eisenhower himself.[7] King was later to confer with Presidents Kennedy and Johnson, as well as with many other national and international figures. A charade of legal stratagems employed by his detractors, and aimed at squelching King's evolving social activism, met with little success. The shining moment of King's leadership came when, on December 10, 1964, at the age of 35, he became the youngest recipient of the Nobel Peace Prize for outstanding contributions to the cause of world peace.[8]

By the time of his death, King had written five books[9] and numerous articles. He had given countless speeches and interviews and preached many sermons. He had crisis-crossed the nation and covered the globe. He had been jailed and physically abused many times. He had advocated many unpopular and disfavored causes. He had been vilified and maligned by his detractors, and adored and adulated by his supporters. Out of this discordant adventure, his message emerged undiluted. It was a message of human and societal healing anchored, as King believed it, in the majestic possibilities of peace, justice, and love for all of God's children, unfettered by diabolic sociocultural forces.

I feel a personal stake in the subject matter of this book. Having grown up under a segregated colonial sociopolitical system, I identified early in life with King's witness and his yearning for a desegregated social system. Having been uprooted at a young age from an intimately supportive extended family environment, my search for a meaningful sense of belonging has been a lifelong quest. King's vision of the beloved community has fed my deepest hunger. Because of King's untimely death, I feel enlisted to contribute to the efforts of those persons who strive to keep alive his lofty dream.

King's witness sought to heal the schizophrenia of a nation whose Declaration of Independence proclaimed an ineffable doctrine of humanity but whose system of justice corroded the noblest instincts. King's witness sought to heal the conflicts of an age that felt discomfited by centuries of wrongs against the disinherited but that felt powerless to change what it deplored. King's witness sought to heal the anguish of those individuals who truly loved justice and peace but felt trapped in a ravenous system and unable to oppose it from within. King's witness sought to heal the agony of those whose daily portion was a crushing one and who cried out for salvation before Jesus' second coming. It spoke to the vocation of pastoral care and counseling, whose mission is to give care to oppressors and oppressed alike, and whose evolving vision is to nurture an inclusive biospheric and anthropologic sense of community.

King was by training neither a pastoral psychologist nor a pastoral theologian. He was trained in systematic theology. However, I believe that the crucible of his work and thought contains valuable insights for practical theology, and that these can be usefully studied for their possible contribution to the vocation of pastoral caregiving with persons from oppressed groups or communities.

Several questions are posed by this book. How does oppression manifest itself in the structures and systems of society? Why is oppression a psychological and theological problem for the oppressed? What are the psychological and theological issues surrounding the phenomena of a tortured self-identity and diminished self-esteem? In what respects are the individualistic counseling models inappropriate for the counseling of oppressed persons who may present tortured self-identity and diminished self-esteem issues? How do King's psychological and theological insights enhance the counseling of persons with these issues? What are the implications of this study for the contemporary vocation of pastoral caregiving and the practice of the Christian ministry?

The elastic aim of the book is to broaden and inform the paradigm for pastoral caregiving as that movement seeks to respond to the needs of the oppressed in any context, especially where Christianity is practiced. In this sense, it is a cross-cultural, intercultural, and transcultural proposal. Yet, it is not socioculturally specific or idiosyncratic; it is oppression sensitive and horizon expansive. It seeks to expand and deepen the vision of the pastoral care movement as it carries out its historical mission of responding to those who hurt and suffer. Inasmuch as the book draws heavily on King's life and witness, it inspires and suggests a prophetic praxis.

A Historical Survey of Pastoral Caregiving

Historically, the counseling vocation has been undergirded by depth philosophies and psychologies. A predominant number of the latter have been the intrapsychic psychologies of the psychoanalytic movement. This movement has largely sought to explicate human psychological and personality development in terms of intrapsychic conflicts and their resolution. This school of thought understands emotional, psychological, and spiritual distress as etiologically rooted in deep-seated and unconscious psychic traumas and conflicts. It has developed intervention strategies consistent with this philosophical and theoretical predisposition.

The natural child of the intrapsychic orientation to psychotherapy is the hyper-individualized, one-on-one intervention modality, wherein distressed individuals or groups seek help in the private offices of trained professionals. These professionals assess and diagnose the presented problem and propose or prescribe its plan of management. The agreed-upon plan is oftentimes developed between the presented and afflicted individual (if an adult), and the professional caregiver. This is a hyperindividualistic model, which many pastoral counselors today continue to practice.

This model of caregiving is characterized by a concentration on distressed individuals or discrete social units, such as families, as the primary focus of assessment, diagnosis, and treatment. This approach to pastoral care and counseling is a carry-over from the days when pastoral care was concerned with the cure of sin-sick souls. The concern was with the individual sufferer or sinner; the focus was on the psyche, understood as mind or soul. The method was probing, inductive, logical, and ethical exhortation. Medicine's preoccupation with trying to find neurologic causes of mental disorders wedded pastoral theology's probes of the psyche with physicians' investigations of the somatic causes of psychic ailments.

> Ever since the 1800s, medical neurologists had assumed responsibility for healing maladies of the soul. But they were struggling to establish themselves as tough-minded empiricists rather than speculative quacks. They were, therefore, inclined to seek a "materialist" solution to every psychic ailment—from back pain to hysteria. They sought tiny anatomical lesions that might cause nervous and mental disorders, or they urged the strengthening of the nervous system.[10]

Through the indefatigable clinical labors and prolific writings of Sigmund Freud, himself a neurologist, psychic disorders were psychologized. This ushered in the psychoanalytic movement. In the United States Anton Boisen, Seward Hiltner, Carroll Wise, and others used the insights of psychoanalytic psychology to develop and further the psychological understanding of human problems in pastoral care and counseling. Their leadership in this area shaped the early stages of the pastoral care and counseling movement in this country. For a long time the theoretical concepts and clinical methods of Freud himself—including those of his detractors and revisionists such as Alfred Adler, Otto Rank, Erich Fromm, Karen Horney, Carl Jung, the existentialists, Erik Erikson, and other neo-Freudians—provided a framework in which pastoral care and counseling were practiced.

In the recent past the dominance of the psychoanalytic orientation has been broadened to include a vision that embraces ecological and other social concerns. Nevertheless, many pastoral counselors today still practice hyperindividualistic caregiving inspired by the theory and methods of depth psychology. Except for instances where the family unit or system is in distress, hyperindividualistic pastoral caregiving focuses on the individual sufferer in its assessment and diagnosis of the presented symptom and in its management. This is done on a case-by-case basis, often in private counseling offices. Even where a family is the presented unit of analysis, hyperindividualistic pastoral caregiving focuses on its idiosyncratic characteristics and individualizes its distress as unique to it.

Unlike the legal and accounting professions, which characterize persons seeking help as clients, or the social work profession, which characterizes them as cases, many pastoral caregivers characterize them as patients. Distressed individuals as well as distressed families are referred to as identified patients. The implications of disease and sickness, reflecting historical antecedents, are apparent in this characterization. The management plans are tailored primarily to distressed individual persons or individual family units. Changing the symptoms of the distress, not necessarily the elimination or eradication of the underlying cause of the distress, is usually the goal of caregiving. The cause of the distress is presumed to be unique and peculiar to the help seekers, and the possible range of etiological factors are presumed to be as varied as the number of help seekers.

Leonard Goodstein and Irwin Sandler write that this hyperindividualistic model of caregiving is passive in that it is the sufferer or his or her representative who must discern the need for help and seek out the caregiver. This is particularly the case where pastoral counseling, contrasted with pastoral care, is concerned. Even when a third-party payer is involved, the contract for services and for their compensation is primarily between the care seeker and the caregiver. The helping process is a private affair between the caregiver and the care seeker, oftentimes in the private offices of the former. The involvement of the sufferer's significant others or the inclusion of a family unit in the therapeutic process does not change the hyperindividualistic and privatistic nature of the process. Pastoral caregiving is most often done away from public view or participation; the individual person or social unit is still the primary focus of assessment, diagnosis, and treatment. Many flaws attend this approach.

Distress common to persons in similar circumstances of time and space is individualized and privatized as to etiology, symptoms, interpretation, and treatment. This often obscures the sociocultural sources of the problem. It imposes guilt and shame on the help seeker. It leaves untreated the toxic and stressing sociocultural forces from whence distressed persons come and to which treated individuals return. It makes it difficult for those most needing help to afford existing services.

Under this hyperindividualistic model, oppressed communities suffer from a paucity of trained professionals. Trained pastoral caregivers are a rarity among oppressed groups. For example, of the 1993 total of 3,187 members of the American Association of Pastoral Counselors (AAPC), only between 25 and 30 were from the ethnic communities of African American, Hispanic, and Asian. This represented only about 0.78 to 0.94 percent of the total membership. For this reason, existing services are not readily accessible or affordable by members of oppressed communities. Many who would benefit from the few available services resist seeing private practitioners. They do not trust them. They dread being labeled sick and carrying this stigma of pathology. For survival reasons in a sociopolitical environment they experience as hostile and dangerous, members of oppressed communities do not wish to divulge their life secrets or personal business to professionals trained in the mainstream culture. Disclosure and divulgence may entail dreadful legal, economic, or political consequences.

Because of its primary focus on the individual, the hyperindividualistic model lacks serious critical social theory and analysis to inform its praxis. Missed is the opportunity for a multisystemic approach to assessment, diagnosis, and intervention. Equally lacking in the hyperindividualistic model are serious justice, peace, and empowerment motifs. Each of these motifs is central to the Christian gospel as the oppressed hear it, and potentially useful for working with those of any community who "labor and are heavy laden." In these motifs seem to intersect the promises of meaningful living and the Gospel.

Concomitantly, the hyperindividualistic model lacks a serious role for the church in its intervention repertoire. The church, as presently constituted and organized, is largely irrelevant to a privatistic, one-on-one counseling model. While the faithful may attend church with no financial hardship, only the financially able have access to counseling. Even for those who can access counseling, there is no guarantee that issues that stem from their faith commitments will receive adequate attention during their counseling sessions. The apparent Sunday-only aliveness of the church renders it unavailable to those seeking help in private offices.

Partly because of these identified flaws, the hyperindividualistic model has received significant challenge from other more socioculturally oriented perspectives. The latter propose different ways of understanding personality development and relationships, and their problematics. These perspectives have developed their own intervention modalities for dealing with disturbed selves and relationships.

Five of these perspectives are: (1) the individual psychology of Alfred Adler, (2) the structural perspective of Salvadore Minuchin, (3) feminist psychologies, (4) ethnic psychologies, and (5) the growth empowerment model of Howard

Clinebell. I believe that these socioculturally oriented perspectives cohere significantly with King's psychological and theological insights on the nature of humans, their development, causes of human distress, and on possible approaches in working with them. I feel that a study of King's thought and work enhances the effectiveness of the pastoral care and counseling vocation for those who can include King's perspectives, particularly those who work with members of oppressed groups. By implication, the pastoral care and counseling models of those whose orientation remains hyperindividualistic can benefit immeasurably from a clear, evocative symbol and prophetic voice for their work, particularly as it pertains to giving care to members of the oppressed groups.

The Nature of the Vocation of Pastoral Care and Counseling

Counseling is the process of enabling a distressed person or group of persons to overcome the symptoms of their distress and achieve wellness or healing. Change of self or of the distressing circumstances is part of the healing process. The distress may be physical or emotional or both. Wellness may be an enhanced form of well-being or the achievement of a homeostatic condition. The physical distress may cause emotional distress, as in post-traumatic emotional syndromes. Conversely, emotional distress may cause physical symptoms, as in psychosomatic illnesses. As a general rule, counseling is employed when the distressing factor is believed to be predominantly emotional and psychological in nature. Effective counseling may alleviate the distress but not necessarily cure its underlying cause.

Pastoral care and counseling is caregiving that draws on the symptom bearer's spiritual or faith resources in symptom management. It is premised on the belief that the Christian faith has efficacious resources to inform and enrich the management of the problem at hand, and to empower the symptom bearer toward restoration or transformation. In this process, symbols or metaphors of God in Christ become central sources of empowerment. While the term "pastoral" may imply that the helper must be an ordained officer of the church, the vocation of pastoral care and counseling is not limited to church officers. It includes lay professionals who, through academic study and clinical training, are deemed to have achieved an integration of the theological and psychological disciplines in their preparation for the vocation of caregiving.

Oppression is the state or condition of being involuntarily dominated or controlled by another. Domination or control of one person or group by another is never consensual. Where consent has been argued to exist—such as in marital, colonial, or enslavement situations—such consent is not informed or is a result of multilayered and multifaceted powerlessness. Oppression itself can be multilevel and multifaceted, encompassing all aspects of the social order and including deep psychological, emotional, and spiritual problems among those affected. Traditional forms of oppression are based on race, gender, and class. In this book, the oppressed groups or communities include the traditional racial groups, and women and the underclass, sometimes referred to as the marginalized. This denotes groups of people who do not participate fully in the wielding of societal power in all its aspects or symbols.

Identity is a person's sense of something called self, and an understanding of who one is in relation to that self and to significant others. It implies a qualitative measure of one's sense of belonging in the social order and a clarified view of the humanity with which a person feels a sense of common personhood or destiny. It also includes one's perception of one's place in the created order, including a belief in a supreme power as creator and governor of all creation. We Christians name that power God. Identity encompasses a felt sense that this supreme power is experienced in ways significantly similar to others like oneself and dissimilar to those unlike oneself.

Powerlessness refers to the actual or apparent inability by a person or group of persons to achieve their desired goals due to obstacles in their path. Actual powerlessness is an objective measure of the inability present in the situation to realize goal achievement. Objective measure can be based on a chronic or transient condition. In either case, the measure is relative to the goal at hand or to the ability of other groups operating in the same time and space to achieve their goals. Apparent powerlessness pertains to a perceived or felt inability, whether or not it is objectively verifiable. The appearance can be from external observation or from within the group. In the latter sense, it can be rooted in the self-esteem of the group. *Empowerment is* the motive force to overcome powerlessness in all the discussed senses. The motive force can spring from the subject group or from an external agency. Empowerment can be sociopolitically, economically, or spiritually grounded.

On the other hand, *praxis* means practice; the pursuit of a vocation as in the practice of ministry or medicine. The conveyed sense is the interactive location of a vocation in time and space. In its sociopolitical sense, praxis is the acting on the existing reality with a view to transforming it. Originated by Paulo Freire and popularized by Gustavo Gutierrez, praxis is a doctrine of liberation theology that teaches that liberation takes place only when the practitioner self-consciously becomes an agent of change, and acts to transform and to be transformed by the reality acted upon.

ONE

———

THE ANATOMY AND PATTERNS OF OPPRESSION

Oppression is demonic. It desecrates the sanctity of life. It corrodes the souls of both oppressed and oppressors. The oppressed are reduced to things. The oppressors are dehumanized by equating their own humanity with the ownership and use of things which include other human beings.

It is helpful to explore the factor of oppression in identity formation and self-esteem among oppressed groups in the United States. We need to address several specific questions. For example, how does oppression manifest itself in the structures and systems of society? In what specific ways does oppression affect identity formation of the poor, women, or the racially nonwhite? How does it affect their self-esteem? Are there discernible common patterns in the way oppression affects the self-esteem and identity formation of members of oppressed groups? What are some of the theological and psychological consequences of oppression among members of the oppressed groups?

This book principally addresses the United States scene. This does not mean or imply that oppression as herein conceived is confined to the U.S. milieu. Global societies share this phenomenon and, wherever necessary, data from other systems are presented to aid conversation or to show common patterns. The limitation is for purposes of subject matter manageability only. Despite the limitation, a typology is established that serves as a useful heuristic device for an understanding of oppression and its specific effects.

Oppression is the sociopolitical phenomenon of inequality. Inequality between persons can usefully be distinguished from inequality of power relations between or among persons. In any given culture or society, persons may be unequal for reasons too many to enumerate. Physical, emotional, spiritual, intellectual or other endowments may render persons unequal. One example of these natural or providential factors that may give rise to inequality is the unequal population densities of the United States, with 267 million people, and the People's Republic of China, with 1.2 billion people.

Another example is the disparate heights of the Pygmies of Central Africa and their neighbors the Tutsi people. Pygmies average about four feet six inches tall, while the Tutsi often reach a height of seven feet. Yet the two groups are considered to be part of the same ethnic group, with a common Bantu language and cultural traditions. Genetic endowment and environmental factors seem to have induced this difference. Oppression, as understood and articulated in this book, does not apply to these natural or providential dissimilitudes.

Our concern is the inequality that is not natural or providential, but which manifests itself in sociocultural power arrangements as a result of unjust use of force, authority, or advantage. This kind of inequality is usually abusive, exploitative, or tyrannical. It seeks its own advantage at the expense of the oppressed and strives to perpetuate itself. In this quest, it employs different devices, with varying degrees of intensity. Some of the common devices used include stereotyping, excluding, underutilizing, underrewarding and miseducating. Each of these devices has been used as a tool for the oppression of women, the racially nonwhite, and the underclass.

The oppression of women is sex-based; that is, women are oppressed because they happen to be female. This is the essence of invidious stereotyping. It is the perpetuation of a belief that a person or group possesses characteristics or qualities that typify that group, and the use of that belief against its members. Stereotyping has been used against women since early biblical times and has, therefore, biblical and theological roots.[1]

Initially, Bible-based stereotyping took the form of the Edenic Fall (Genesis 2:15–17), which supposedly explains Adam's estrangement from God. The female, Eve, is blamed for this estrangement. She supposedly allowed the serpent to beguile her into sinning against the glory of God, and enticed Adam to participate in this sinful act. This event, which gave birth to the theological doctrine of original sin, is blamed on the innate sinfulness of the female.[2] The Edenic Fall gave rise to the stereotypic image of women as congenitally lustful, morally depraved, and spiritually unfit.

Mary Daly writes that prominent theologians have sought to justify female oppression as a means of managing women's presumed innate depravity. She quotes the preeminent theologian Tertullian of Carthage as fulminating about women:

> You are the devil's gateway . . . How easily you destroyed man, the image of God. Because of the death which you brought upon us, even the Son of God had to die.[3]

Daly cites theologians James Sprenger and Heinrich Kraemer as agreeing that "all witchcraft comes from carnal lust, which is in women insatiable."[4] The hunting and burning of witches that took place in Europe from the fourteenth through the seventeenth centuries has been traced to this original sin stereotyping of the female.[5]

The subjugation of women also has been justified by the creation story stereotype. The female is viewed as God's defective copy of the male, deficient in many respects and subordinate to the male. John Calvin's perspective on this issue is telling:

> Since in the person of the man the human race had been created, the common dignity of our whole nature was without distinction . . . The woman . . . was nothing else than

an accession to the man . . . We may therefore conclude that, the order of nature implies that the woman should be the helper of the man. The vulgar proverb, indeed, is that she is a necessary evil . . . that the woman is given as a companion and associate to the man, to assist him to live well.[6]

This religio-theological stereotyping of women as innately sinful can complicate identity formation and self-esteem among women. As bearer of responsibility for original sin according to this doctrine, the female can view herself as the embodi-  ment of that which is defective, deficient, wrong, and degenerate about society and culture. This self-deprecation can also lead to complicity in the woman's own oppression as a form of psychological penance.

Nineteenth-century social theories predicated on Darwinism did not fail to lend support to the stereotyping of women begun in biblical times and perpetuated by some Christian theologians. Charles Darwin (1809–1882) propounded a theory of the origin of species that saw a relentless evolution characterized by the survival of the fittest and the extinction of the unfit. When these ideas were extended to human social phenomena in a theory called social Darwinism, they were used to justify unequal treatment of women due to their presumed biological and intellectual feebleness. Women's function in conception and motherhood was used to justify relegating them to domestic duties, thus depriving them of equal participation in significant social roles.[7]

Twentieth-century Freudian psychology crowned the genderization of male and female sex differences begun by social Darwinism. According to Freud, female biology was destiny.[8] By this Freud meant that women's behavior was due to their sex, not to their status in society, and was rooted in female penis envy and castration complex. Little girls between ages three and six suffered psychological trauma when they discovered that they lacked penises. This feeling of lack forever doomed the female to feelings of perpetual deficiency and inferiority. This felt deficiency affected women's personality, as well as their ethical development.

Freud stated, "I cannot evade the notion . . . that for women the level of what is ethically normal is different from what it is in men."[9] In this way Freudian psychology, which for a long time reigned supreme and continues to play a major role in the psychological study of human behavior, genderizes women's behavior as stereotypically abnormal and inferior. Not social status but deficient, abnormal, and inferior sexuality is to blame. Males, themselves products of Freudian psychology, use this stereotyping to justify the belief that they are inherently superior to women and to act on that belief.

The female who experiences oppression today at the hands of male culture is not the same female who was created by God but the woman invented by the male culture through the use of theological, scientific, and psychological theories. These theories seek to ascribe certain innate biological characteristics to her that themselves are the invention and perpetuation of dominant male culture. The end product is a feminized female whose identity and behavior seek to mirror the stereotypes imposed on her by the male. She bears characteristics that male culture both hates and employs to justify oppressing the female.

Title VII of the U.S. Civil Rights Act of 1964, as amended, prohibits discrimination against people in employment based on many criteria, one of which is sex.[10] Thus, women are covered by the law. "Discrimination" is the law's word for disequalization, the intentional and disparate treatment of persons based on their stereotypic characteristics. In enacting this legislation proscribing discrimination in the workplace, congress mirrored the political conscience of the nation by acknowledging that women were being economically oppressed by being excluded, underutilized, or underpaid. However, despite legislative prohibition, there is continuing evidence of economic oppression and exploitation of women.

In 1989, 25 years after passage of Title VII of the Civil Rights Acts of 1964, over 56 million women aged 16 years and over were in the civilian labor force. This constituted over 58 percent of the total labor force.[11] Of this percentage, only about 25.2 percent held managerial and professional positions. Only 1.7 percent of the women in this group earned $50,000 or more per year, compared with 11.7 percent of the men. In general, women in the United States earn about 66 cents for every dollar earned by men doing the same or similar work.[12] Clearly, women did not choose to endure these economic disparities. The fact that these disparities exist stems from systematic disequalization by the male power structure.

The status of women in the political sphere is no more reassuring. Even though in 1989, women accounted for 51 percent of the U.S. population (127 million women versus 121 million males),[13] there are today only six women senators out of a total of 100, and only 47 women in the House of Representatives out of a total of 431. The exclusion of women from the seat of political power is evident from the additional fact that there has been no female president or vice president in the history of the United States.

Worldwide, in the twentieth century, only the following sixteen countries have had female elected heads of state or government: the Philippines, Iceland, Nicaragua, Haiti, Bolivia, Argentina, Irish Republic, the United Kingdom, the Netherlands Antilles, Dominica, Grenada, Norway, India, Sri Lanka, Israel, Portugal, and Pakistan.[14] Again worldwide, only 10 percent of high government officials are women, and only 5 percent of the corporate executive officers are women.[15]

In the area of ecclesiastical leadership, many Protestant denominations have only recently begun ordaining women. The Roman Catholic church, with a worldwide membership of more than 950 million, does not ordain women to the priesthood, rendering relatively powerless the majority of its membership. The reason for this exclusion is a belief in the unfitness of women to serve male deities, God in Christ, in high offices. It is believed that women, by reason of their sex alone, are unable to

represent or symbolize Jesus in the priesthood. The January 1977 Va
tion makes this point explicitly when it states:

> It is this ability to represent Christ that St. Paul considered as characteri.
> apostolic function . . . . The supreme expression of this representation is fou... in the
> altogether special form it assumes in the celebration of the eucharist, which is the
> source and center of the church's unity, the sacrificial meal in which the people of God
> are associated in the sacrifice of Christ; the priest, who alone has the power to perform
> it, then acts not only through the effective power conferred on him by Christ, but *in
> persona Christi*, taking the role of Christ, to the point of being his very image, when he
> pronounces the words of consecration . . . . The same natural resemblance is required
> for persons as for things: when Christ's role in the eucharist is to be expressed sacra-
> mentally, there would not be this "natural resemblance" which must exist between
> Christ and his minister if the role of Christ were not taken by a man; in such a case it
> would be difficult to see in the minister the image of Christ. For Christ was and
> remains a man . . . . The Church, in fidelity to the example of the Lord, does not con-
> sider herself authorized to admit women to priestly ordination.[16]

From this passage it is evident that the priesthood is premised on the belief that
males are closer to God in Christ than females, that they are God's representatives
on earth, or lesser gods themselves. Indeed, feminist theologian Mary Daly has
argued that the maleness of God implies that "the male is God."[17] Such a view lends
additional theological justification to the oppression of the female by the male, and
can intensify the problem of self-concept (identity) and feelings of self-worth (self-
esteem) in the female. A theology that locates one segment of humanity closer to
the divine than another implies a hierarchical ordering of society. The male is perceived as divinely ordained to be superior to the female. Such indeed was the position taken in 1962 by a Roman Catholic scholar, Emmanuel Doronzo.[18]

One response an oppressed group makes in an effort to alleviate its oppression is
to seek educational goals. The attainment of these goals is believed to enable them
to effectively participate in the oppressive system, to better understand and deal
with it, or to commend themselves as acceptable individuals to the oppressor.
Women have tried this strategy with marginal success.

Women have by and large been excluded from serious educational opportunities
on grounds that they are both too emotional and intellectually deficient to cope
successfully with the rigors of study. It has also been argued that educational pur-
suits would render them unsuitable partners for men, that is, unsuitable to serve
men. As a consequence, in the early days of the founding of this republic, girls were
allowed to attend school only in the summer when boys were on vacation or
employed. The curriculum was severely modified in order to produce wifely assis-
tants to men. Only arts and religious courses were emphasized.[19]

Globally, 63 percent of the more than 900 million illiterates are women. Some regions have higher than 70 percent illiteracy rates for women aged 25 and over.[20] Consequently, women are undereducated, underemployed, and underpaid. Psychologically, "women have been conditioned to want less, to expect less, and to receive less than men do." This psychological sense of self-denial, self-abnegation, and self-deprecation is one manifestation of female oppression, and can have negative effects on identity formation and self-esteem.

Anthropologists have classified the human race into three major racial groups: the Caucasoid, Negroid, and Mongoloid races. This classification may not be truly inclusive of all the possible racial groups on earth. For instance, it is not clear how the Native American people fit into this classification. In the same vein, Egyptians have variously been classified either as Caucasian or Negroid, depending on the prevailing political winds of classificatory science. In this book, the racially nonwhite refers to the Negroid and Mongoloid groups. Methods of oppressing women on the basis of sex have been employed for oppression of nonwhite groups as well. Even though the discussion will focus primarily on the oppression of blacks worldwide, it is understood that racially motivated oppression has common features across the racially nonwhite groups.

The oppression of blacks has historically been justified on the grounds that they are the descendants of the biblical Ham, whose story is told in Genesis 9:18–27. This pericope is the racial counterpart to the Edenic Fall of women's oppression. The cited text establishes Ham as the father of Canaan. Ham commits an indiscretion concerning his father's sexuality. He sees him naked and apparently humorizes the episode. When his father Noah awakens from his drunken state and is told about Ham's behavior, he blesses Ham's brothers Shem and Japheth to prosper and curses Ham's son Canaan to be their slave (Genesis 9:25–27). In Genesis 10:6–20, all the descendants of Ham are named, and the list includes Canaan, Cush, Put, and Egypt. By some strange exegetical logic, the Hamitic theory identified Ham and his descendants as black people who were biblically cursed to serve the white descendants of Shem and Japheth.[22] Some biblicists have justified the enslavement and oppression of blacks on the basis of this hypothesis.

The application of this hypothesis has not been historically consistent. When it has suited the oppressors' purposes, the hypothesis has been revised to exclude the people of Egypt and, sometimes, Ethiopia as Ham's descendants by classifying them as part of the white race.

> During the course of centuries, upon the basis of the Bible the black man has been viewed in several and various ways. He has been regarded as the veritable father of Eastern civilizations; as cursed of God or by a prophetic man of God, forever destined to serve his more favored brethren. . . . At the same time, but still upon the basis of the Bible, he has . . . [been] . . . declared to be a beast . . . [and] to cause . . . the disinte-

gration and decay of ancient civilizations. . . . Then, around 1800, a new stream came to the surface. This . . . new Hamite Hypothesis, eliminates the black man from the biblical world. Those black peoples whom it retains are given the title Caucasoid Blacks who instead of being regarded as Negroes are viewed as being white.[23]

In a similar vein, the injunction in Colossians 3:22–25 that slaves should obey their masters, attributed to Paul, was used by slavemasters to indicate divine approval of slavery in the United States. Instructional materials were produced that sought to brainwash slaves into believing that God approved their submission to enslavement and oppression.

> All slaves were inculcated with the idea that whites ruled from God and that to question this white divine-right theory was to incur the wrath of heaven, if not to call for a more immediate sign of displeasure here below. A slave was told that his condition was the fulfillment of the will of the master on high.[24]

In a manner reminiscent of the scientific justification for the inferiority and oppression of women, scientific and pseudoscientific theories on race were used to justify slavery and the oppression of black people from the seventeenth through the early twentieth centuries, and became a bulwark for white supremacy. The spread of social Darwinism after 1900 furnished a "scientific" basis for ranking races, with blacks at the bottom. The development of IQ tests in the twentieth century, and their use to measure intelligence, confirmed the theory of the inferiority of black people.

White anthropologists sought to confirm these scientific theories by arguing that the cranial capacities of blacks were smaller than those of whites, denoting that blacks had smaller brains than white people. These so-called scientific theories sought to stereotype the black race as innately and genetically inferior, justifying oppressive treatment.[25] Psychological theories rooted in studies of intelligence and behavior by William Shockley have sought to confirm this stereotype.[26]

Evidence abounds that scientific and psychological theories used to explain black inferiority and justify the oppression of blacks were latter-day European American inventions. They do not describe early contacts between Europeans and black people on the African continent. Early sixteenth-century European traders had high regard for black men and women and for African institutions. On their way to India, these traders stopped over in Africa to replenish their water supply and provisions. Early contacts between the two peoples occurred on the basis of mutual respect, not on the presumptions of African cultural inferiority. Indeed, Africa was esteemed for its economic abundance. This positive dynamic between Africans and Europeans soured as the latter sought to maximize their triangular profits between Europe, Africa, and America, and saw human merchandise as more profitable than goods.[27]

The exclusion of black people from meaningful participation in international economic life begun during the enslaving and slavery eras continues today. During the enslaving period, the mid-fifteenth through the nineteenth centuries, an estimated 60 million to 100 million Africans were imported to the United States.[28] African social, economic, and political orders were severely disrupted during the 400 years of social violence that attended the capture of slaves. No meaningful economic activity was possible between 1445 and 1870. The population of Africa stagnated at 100 million people between 1650 and 1850 and only rose to 120 million after enslaving violence ceased. In comparison, the population of Europe rose from 103 million in 1850 to 423 million in 1900.[29] The slave traders captured only the most able-bodied young men and women between ages 15 and 35, with the majority in their teens and twenties, leaving African societies depleted of essential economic labor. While African societies deteriorated, the profits to the slave traders soared.

> By this triangular system, three separate profits were taken, and all in Europe: the first profit was that of selling consumer goods to the slaves; the second derived from selling slaves to the planters and mine owners of the Americas; while the third (and biggest) was realized on the sale of American and West Indian cargoes in Europe.[30]

Africa remains the most impoverished and oppressed of all the continents. African Americans were severely pauperized and remain so today.

The economic oppression of African Americans begun in enslaving times takes a different form today. While during slavery the African American was overemployed but undercompensated, today he is largely unemployed, underemployed, and underpaid. The African American community lives in a state of chronic economic depression compared to its white counterpart.

In 1990, the African American unemployment rate was 12.6 percent, while the European American unemployment rate in 1990 was 5.1 percent.[31] African Americans with bachelor's degrees earn less than European Americans with high-school diplomas. African American high-school graduates earn less than European American eighth-grade dropouts.[32] African American families earn 57 percent of what European American families earn.[33]

In 1987, 33 percent of African American families lived below the poverty level, compared with only 10.5 percent of European American families.[34] Lastly, 97 percent of all physicians and dentists and 98 percent of all psychiatrists and psychologists are European American.[35] That the exclusion from meaningful economic participation is used as an oppressive tool can be gleaned from the presented data.

During slavery days, African Americans enjoyed no human or civil rights. They were mere chattel; they did not even own themselves. They could not own property, testify in courts of law, marry, control their own children, vote, or run for elective office. Their exclusion from the political process was absolute. The Supreme Court decision in *Dred Scott v. Sandford* (1857) confirmed this.[36]

Following ratification of the Thirteenth, Fourteenth, and Fifteenth Amendments to the U.S. Constitution, African Americans enjoyed some measure of participation in the political process, and ran for elective offices in local, state, and federal elections. This occurred during the Reconstruction era, when the hopes of the ex-slaves for full membership in American society were raised. But these hopes were dashed by the resurgence of intense racial oppression and repression represented by the Ku Klux Klan and the Jim Crow laws, which replaced slavocracy with segregation laws. Where segregation did not exist de jure, as in many parts of the nation other than the Deep South, it existed de facto. The U.S. Supreme Court decision in *Plessy v. Ferguson* (1896), promulgating the doctrine of "separate but equal" accommodations, legitimized both de jure and de facto segregation. Intensified separation, and less equality, ensued.

The passage of the Voting Rights Act of 1965 increased African American participation in electoral politics. Because of this, African American office holding at all levels of government increased from 280 African American elected officials in 1965 to over 6,000 by 1985. Nevertheless, this figure represented only 1.2 percent of all elected officials in the country.[37] It is significant that there is currently no African American governor or lieutenant governor, and in the area of national office holding, there is only one senator (Carol Moseley-Braun from Illinois) and only 39 representatives in the U.S. Congress. A 1990 attempt by an African American to win a Senate seat from North Carolina failed. Jesse Jackson's 1984 and 1988 forays into presidential politics failed. No African American has served as a presidential running mate. The significance of all this is the degree to which the nation continues to exclude African Americans from significant seats of national and international power, where both visibility and actual policy making have immense symbolic significance. Visible participation would elevate African American leaders from being perceived as primarily, if not exclusively, civil rights and ghetto leaders to national and international leadership. They would be able to claim their place among similar leaders. It would end their degrading confinement to narrow, parochial, racial or single-issue expertise. It would gain them wider national and international respect and develop their comfort level and sophistication with the acquisition, wielding, and use of power. Not only would this enhance their stature as statesmen among global communities, it would enhance their roles as models to their communities and youth and help heal the endemic feelings of worthlessness among many African Americans. Participation and role visibility would deepen the sense of ownership of the American dream by the African American community and help melt some of the felt rage at being excluded, marginalized, disvalued, and abused.

An examination of the spiritual leadership of this nation offers no relief from its secular pattern of exclusion as a tool of marginalization and oppression. African American exclusion from significant ecclesiastical leadership is no less intense or obtuse. The complexity of the problem mirrors the strange and complicated nature of American religious life. It can be argued that there is considerable African American ecclesiastical leadership in this nation, but only if one significant fact is noted: Most of this leadership evolved as a response to the segregated nature of American Christianity and is confined to the African American community. The American Christian church is the most segregated institution in American society. Vastly more citizens work together Monday through Friday than worship together on Sunday. That is, there is more integration in the workplace than in the Lord's house. As Christians, we have lived and continue to live with the frightening reality that the church, which evolved to preach and preaches the gospel of human sorority and fraternity, is essentially apostate. It incubates, fosters, and festers incalculable intolerance and hatred. European Americans and African Americans can hardly worship together. Each time the two races join to celebrate the gospel of Jesus Christ under the same roof, the European Americans eventually flee, leaving behind them previously owned sanctuaries and, in some cases, exhuming their dead. It is little wonder that the unchurched world looks on with sarcasm and bemused interest. The Christian church is not able to model the kind of love it preaches, for which Jesus died, and which the world desperately needs.

While some African American Christians worship in racially mixed congregations, vastly more worship in segregated congregations of constitutionally integrated denominations, and in segregated congregations within segregated denominations. The current reality springs from the historical fact that the universalism of the Christian gospel did not extend to African Americans. During the slavery era, this led to the evolution of the "invisible institution" of worship among the enslaved.[38] Because they were excluded from the meaningful worship of God, African Americans founded their own congregations. The most illustrious example was the organization by Richard Allen and Absalom James of the Free African Society in 1787, which eventuated in the founding of Richard Allen's AME Bethel Church in 1794.

Independent African American church denominations mushroomed from this momentous event, and African American worship took on a distinctively different form.[39] Thus, the European American church—which wields immense social, political, and economic power—is the most segregated institution in this society. African Americans play no significant role in its governance or mission. Until recently, this scenario was replicated internationally, where mission churches had been established by Euro-American missionary societies, and this is still clearly the case in South Africa.

Denial of educational opportunities to oppressed groups is another oppressive tool, and this denial takes three forms: actual refusal to provide schools for the subject people; provision of separate and inferior schools; or miseducating the oppressed.[40] The African American community has endured all three of these forms.

While slaves were considered chattel, it was philosophically and legally impossible to contemplate educating them. Poor European American boys were apprenticed into trades and wealthy European American boys were offered Latin grammar schools as early as 1600.[41] Slaves were not, and it was illegal to offer them any type of schooling.

Public education for European American boys and girls was established throughout the states by 1875.[42] Except for the post-Emancipation founding of segregated colleges in the South by Northern philanthropists, the United States has never as a nation seriously committed itself to the education of African Americans. As an enslaved person, the African American was taught to take orders from any European American but not to give any, and to de-Africanize without re-Americanizing. His destiny was to produce for the white American, not for himself (or herself).[43]

Not educating African Americans has been justified on the grounds that they are both uneducable or too dangerous to educate. Educating them in separate and inferior schools historically served to break their identity as human beings so that they could accept their subordinated position.[44] The report of the National Advisory Commission on Civil Disorders, requested by President Lyndon B. Johnson following the ghetto riots of 1967, echoes this sentiment when it states:

> As Americans, most Negro citizens carry within themselves two basic aspirations of our society. They seek to share in both the material resources of our system and its intangible benefits—dignity, respect and acceptance. . . . Pervasive discrimination and segregation . . . surely . . . [excludes] . . . great numbers of Negroes from the benefits of economic progress through discrimination in employment and education, and their enforced confinement in segregated housing and schools. The corrosive and degrading effects of this condition and the attitudes that underlie it are the source of the deepest bitterness and at the center of the problem of racial disorder. . . . The racial attitude and behavior of white Americans . . . white racism . . . is essentially responsible for the explosive mixture which has been accumulating in our cities since the end of World War II.[45]

At the time of King's assassination in 1968, the percentage of African American males admitted into United States prisons relative to the total prison population was 35 percent, compared with 44 percent today;[46] this despite the fact that African American males constitute only 5.5 percent of the U.S. population. Overall, the United States incarcerates a higher rate of African American males per 100,000 of the population (3,370) than did the apartheid regime of South Africa (681).[47] Based on the total national population, the United States in 1989 incarcerated 23 percent of its African American citizens, compared with 10.4 percent Hispanic and 6.2 percent of European Americans.[48]

The poor or the underclass as an oppressed group face identity and self-esteem problems that are unique to their status and deserve particular examination. For example, Latin American liberation theology has developed formidable scholarship around them and their reality. But who are these people?

By and large, they are members of the same groups that have been examined thus far—women and racial minorities. While it is true that the poor include European Americans, it is also true that the vast majority of the poor, relative to their respective populations, are racial minorities and the women of any group.

For instance, of the conservative figure of 13.5 percent of all races who were classified poor in 1990, 10.7 percent were European American, 28.1 percent were Hispanic American, and 31.9 percent were African American.[49] Of the population-wide 10.7 percent rate for families living below the poverty level in 1990, the rate for households headed by single European American males was only 9.9 percent, compared to 26.8 percent for households headed by single European American females. The rate for families headed by single African American males was only 20.4 percent compared to 48.1 percent for households headed by single African American females. The rate for households headed by single Hispanic males was only 19.4 percent compared to over 40 percent for households headed by single Hispanic females.[50]

It can be seen that households headed by single females of each racial group were vastly poorer than those headed by males. Households headed by single African American or Hispanic males were vastly poorer than those headed by single European American males. Households headed by single African American or Hispanic females were vastly poorer than those headed by single European American females. In short, households headed by a single non–European American person, male or female, were vastly poorer than those headed by a European American.

In talking about the poor or the underclass it seems more correct to use the term *ethclass* to describe (denote) the point at which social class and ethnic group membership intersect.[51] This term of reference also appropriately acknowledges the dual reality facing ethnic group members, that even though they may succeed economically and materially, they still do not achieve full acceptance by the dominant middle-class European American system. It is in this sense that the materially successful belong to the oppressed *ethclass* with which a part of this book is concerned.

We can see how stereotyping and exclusion have been used as instruments of oppression of persons not European American. The excursion began in the biblical world of the so-called Hamitic theory, as explained above, and has extended to scientific, psychological, economic, political, ecclesiastical, and educational forces that have been arrayed against these people. Even though the discussion has focused largely on the African Americans in the United States, its heuristic value is validated by the fact that this group comprises the largest block of non–European Americans in the nation. It is also the most fully non–European American. Other groups occupy positions of varying degrees of non-Europeanism ranging from almost completely European American to almost completely non–European American, or African American.

The Hispanics, for instance, are classifiable by the Census Bureau as either African American or European American, depending on how much blood of either race they have in their veins. The degree and extent to which each of these non–European American groups suffers oppression seems to depend on the degree of their non-Europeanism and the historical circumstances attending their residence in the United States.[52]

Nevertheless, the heuristic utility of examining the African American experience is validated by the fact that whether one talks about African Americans, Asian/Pacific Island Americans, Native Americans, or Hispanic Americans, factors contributing to their oppression include their ethnic minority status and the impact of external European American system on their minority cultures concerning issues such as biculturalism, ethnicity and language, ethnicity and social class.[53] The term *ethclassism* seems appropriate to describe the oppression of the racially non–European Americans, the majority of whom suffer the disabilities of racial, economic and cultural imperialism.

The Factor and Consequences of Oppression in Identity Formation

The issue of how oppression might influence identity formation is intimately connected with the question of how oppression might affect the *core of personality*, for identity formation is a central part of personality and its development. Identity can usefully be equated with a sense of self or self-concept. Personality development can therefore be conceptualized as the study of how identity or sense of self or self-concept forms and develops. This is the approach followed in this book.

It is helpful to distinguish between the core of personality and the periphery of personality. The former, core of personality, refers to those aspects of personality that are presumed to be universal to all people and are inherent attributes of human beings. These common features do not change much in the course of living, and exert an extensive, pervasive influence on behavior.[54] The periphery of personality pertains to those attributes of personality that are generally learned, not inherent, and have a relatively circumscribed influence on behavior.[55] The distinction Salvatore Maddi draws between these two attributes of personality can be equated with what Daniel Lapsley and Kenneth Rice have usefully referred to as the ontological and epistemological aspects of personality.[56] The ontological attribute of personality can therefore be viewed as the *beingness* of the person, the *I amness* of identity. The epistemological can be viewed as the *becomingness* of personality, the attribute of identity that is self-causing and intentional, sets boundaries, and fulfills the potentialities inherent in the ontological.[57]

The oppression of women, non–European Americans, and the underclass affects both their ontological and epistemological bases of personality as herein proposed. In a social and theological milieu that prescribes that the oppressed are nonpersons or subhumans, the question of *beingness* or *I amness* of the oppressed is as conflicted and fractured as is the question of what I am to become.

Because of the theological and psychological presumption of female defectiveness, a woman can conceivably see herself as an incomplete human being who needs a man to complete her. Her identity can depend on the validation of the normative male, not that of oneself, other females, or God. She can identify as an understudy or an assistant human, not as a competent one, capable of proactivity and self-agency. She can identify as a symbol or an idea, in the sense that society has invented the idea or symbol of her and deals with that, not with the real human being that she is. That is, she can identify as a male-defined caricature, not as a real, self-defined and God created person.[58]

She can identify as an object and a victim, passive and receptive, not as a subject of her own biography and history. She can identify as other-directed not as self-directed, thus feeling alienated from true self and others. She can identify as a pseudo self, with a diminished integrity of self. She can engage in idolatry by glorifying maleness, not the true God, by regarding the sinful male as the normative human against whom to measure her self worth and perfectibility instead of a God given standard of infinite worth and potential. She can commit the sin of submitting to, instead of resisting, oppression, which is unholy and ungodly. The sinful male can become her demigod, thus distorting the true essence of God.

Indeed, Helen Deutsch, a disciple of Freud, attributed what she regarded as women's submissive identity to what she called their instinctual sexual wish and masochism.[59] It took Karen Horney to argue the contrary; that what may have appeared to be female submissiveness and masochism may have been a complex response to issues of powerlessness, fear, and a striving for safety in the face of male hostility, aggression, and oppression.[60] She argued that what male society had interpreted as an inherent tendency of the woman for concupiscence and moral depravity may also have been adaptive behavior to feelings of powerlessness and the need for safety or security from male aggression.

Freud had observed that "for women the level of what is ethically normal is different from what it is in men. Their superego is never so inexorable, so impersonal, so independent of emotional origins as we require it to be in men."[61] He may have been correct in his observation that women's developmental course and their resolution of ethical issues differed from men's, but he erred in his explanation that what he saw was female deficiency occasioned by penis envy.

Some writers have referred to the identity phenomenon Freud was describing as (1) powerless femininity, (2) woman who mistakes herself for a man, (3) man-made woman, (4) woman as victim, or (5) woman with a fractured or conflicted sense of self.

Miriam Greenspan states the problem in this way:

> The raw data upon which Freud drew his conclusions about female psychology were the conflicts that women had about being normal women. Indeed, many of his female patients were engaged in both overt and covert rebellions against normal womanhood. . . . The Freudian norm of femininity in which woman is seen as an incomplete and mutilated man is a single reflection of woman's traditional dilemma: <u>to be a woman, she must behave as a mutilated person</u>; to be a person she must see herself, and be seen by others, as a woman who mistakes herself for a man. . . . In this sense, woman has always been socialized to be woman as victim.[62]

[margin annotation: relate to this]

Harriet Goldhor Lerner refers to the sense of self described by Greenspan as de-selfed self or pseudo self, an identity wrought of an inner fear of being fully human or fully self for fear of offending the fragility of the male ego.[63] Anne Wilson Schaef calls women's fragmented and incomplete sense of self the Original Sin of Being Born Female.[64] She explicates the Original Sin as women's feeling of incompleteness without a male anchor.

> Many women feel that they cannot be whole without a man. . . . Women are often terrified of being alone. Being "connected" to someone else—a man—ensures their survival. They do not understand that even when no one else is around they are still with someone—themselves. . . . <u>We are taught that we will be all right if we can only attach ourselves to an innately superior being, a man, who will intercede for us.</u>[65]

[margin annotation: authentic family culture]

This passage hints at the extreme forms of self-abnegation and fracturedness, in addition to the idolatry of male worship, that can distort worship of the true God.

The insights of feminist psychologists discussed in this chapter may seem to raise questions about the claims of those feminist psychologists who have sought to challenge the distortions of the Freudian view of female identity formation with their own paradigm of relationality. The question is whether female identity that seeks its normativity in being-in-relationship is necessarily sex-based, rather than a gender-ized construct. That is, is the sense of self sought in relationships normative to the biological fact of being female, or is it due to the terror of aloneness, which in turn is due to the felt oppression of being born female? Jean Baker Miller calls this oppressive factor <u>permanent inequality</u>.[66]

Miller asserts as normative the view that women's identity derives from maintaining affiliations and relationships.

Indeed, women's sense of self becomes very much organized around being able to make and then to maintain affiliations and relationships. . . . For many women the threat of disruption of connections is perceived not just as a loss of relationship but as something closer to a total loss of self. . . . Affiliation is valued as highly as, or more highly than, self-enhancement.[67]

While this suggests a way of assessing identity formation in women in contradistinction to that in men, it raises the question of whether the affiliative and relational tendency of self-definition in women is a core (ontological) characteristic of being female or a periphery (epistemological) characteristic of femaleness. If the latter, then there is some question as to whether a methodology rooted in a tendency that is adaptive to the factor of oppression can yield a true picture of female identity formation. Does not the true female remain unknown and unknowable?

Carol Gilligan, among others, has argued that from infancy female personality development is oriented toward connectedness and attachment to others and to the ethic of care. She posits that attachment and connectedness are distinct female characteristics that differ markedly from dominant male characteristics, which center on the ethic of justice. "While an ethic of justice proceeds from the premise of equality—that everyone should be treated the same—an ethic of care rests on the premise of non-violence—that no one should be hurt."[68] Gilligan adds:

The concept of identity expands to include the experience of interconnection. The moral domain is similarly enlarged by the inclusion of responsibility and care in relationships. . . . As we have listened for centuries to the voices of men and the theories of development that their experience informs, so we have come more recently to notice not only the silence of women but the difficulty of hearing what they say when they speak.[69]

Gilligan seems to assume that this predisposition of females toward connectedness, attachment, and relationship is an inherent (ontological), core characteristic of being female that requires a different understanding of female development. However, if this characteristic is primarily and largely adaptive, Gilligan's assumption leaves unanswered the question of the uniqueness of female development in the absence of oppression. For example, in what unique ways would this female characteristic manifest itself if sex-based oppression were absent? Whether it would change or not, and in what unique ways, remains an open question.

The issue of identity or sense of self plaguing female individuals parallels that of the racially oppressed inasmuch as the structures of oppression are similar between the two groups. In each instance an oppressor's theory was involved. These theories range from biblical, to scientific, to psychological stereotyping. Exclusion from participation is involved. Oppression of the racially nonwhite has been rationalized in ways similar to the rationalization of the oppression of women. Assumptions of innate racial and genetic inferiority have been employed as the respective theories. These theories do not exist only in the mind as speculative or conjectural points of view; in their oppressive tenets, these theories take on the quality of ideologies, ideas that infuse a whole culture and that shape political and social arrangements. Sexism is one such ideology; racism is yet another. Let us now look at the anatomy and consequences of racism more closely.

A useful definition of racism is offered by Theo Witvliet in his book *A Place in the Sun.*

> Racism is the specific ideology which organizes and regulates the exploitation and dependence of a particular race (group, people) on the basis of the supposed cultural and/or biological inferiority of this "race," and in this way perpetuates and deepens already existing differences of power.[70]

Witvliet makes clear that racism as an ideology is not a head trip. One need not think racist thoughts in order to act in a racist manner. One need only be shaped by a racist environment; for racism "finds its expression in the total social reality in which we are involved as individuals—in institutions like churches, schools and law courts, and also in architecture and music. As such it precedes the individual and forms his or her world, determining what is taken for granted within that world."[71] Witvliet shows how easily one can become a racist or behave in a racist fashion without conscious thought or intention.

Frantz Fanon, a black psychiatrist and philosopher from Martinique, dealt specifically with the psychological problems of the racially and colonially oppressed. He discovered that the identities of the colonized blacks suffered serious fracture once they came in contact with the white culture.

> As long as the black man is among his own, he will have no occasion, except in minor internal conflicts, to experience his being through others. There is of course the moment of "being for others," of which Hegel speaks, but every ontology is made unattainable in a colonized and civilized society. . . . Ontology—once it is finally admitted as leaving existence by the wayside—does not permit us to understand the being of the black man. For not only must a black man be black; he must be black in relation to the white man.[72]

Fanon discovered that a colonized black person was psychologically split. He behaved differently around white people than around his fellow blacks. He did everything possible to impress and please a white person. He tried to imitate the language, lifestyle, and folkways of white people. In short, he deculturated himself from his authentic native culture and strove to reacculturate into white ways of being. He wanted to be white, and tried to become so. In the process he was at risk to annihilate his true self, his ego-identity.

When the Negro makes contact with the white world, a certain sensitizing action takes place. If his psychic structure is weak, one observes a collapse of the ego. The black man stops behaving as an *actional* person. The goal of his behavior will be The Other (in the guise of a white man), for The Other alone can give him worth . . . self-esteem.[73]

We have just seen how, in connection with female identity, this can be an aspect of de-selfing, and an ontological abandonment of the self. For the female, this abandonment can be a consequence of the introjection of the male value system, which teaches and conditions that the male is the normative human being and the female only a defective copy. Of course Fanon was writing in an oppressive colonial context. He discovered that, even in that context, the natives felt and believed that to be truly human one had to mimic the ways of being of the colonial master, who had created systems and structures rewarding those who conformed and penalizing those who did not.

Over a period of time, this subtle and sometimes violent coercion gave way to submission to and acceptance of the new reality. Acceptance was achieved by an introjection of a foreign value system and a simultaneous depreciation of the indigenous value system. Force often was employed to impose the new order, but not always. Educational, religious, health care and even recreational institutions were employed as devices. These were subtle but equally potent psychological tools of deculturation and reacculturation. For example, golf, tennis, soccer, rugby, and cricket replaced dance as the acceptable forms of civilized recreation. In Africa, the monotheistic conception of God was imposed and supplanted the panentheistic African conception.

There might appear to be dissimilarities between female de-selfing and colonial deculturation. One takes place within an indigenous sociocultural milieu and does not require foreign agency for its effectuation. The other, colonial, does require such an agency. But a closer look reveals a pattern that is relevant and applicable to both situations as an analytical aid. For instance, if images of self and identity are understood as culturally shaped instead of simply intrapsychic, then it is doubtful that a deculturated individual can enjoy authentic self-identity. He would experience a refracted self-identity that is a hybrid of indigenous and foreign. Indeed, it is for this reason that the offspring of Europeans and Africans in Africa are called "half-castes."

It is also for this reason that deculturation can be a type of de-selfing; it can be an impoverished way of achieving self-identity and a tortured way of contributing to, and feeling secure in, a reproduction of culture that shapes identity. Feminists point out that female introjection of male images of self and identity de-selfs them and impoverishes their creative contributions to culture. Fanon makes a similar case for the colonially oppressed. Inasmuch as, theologically, idolatry can be a real problem for the de-selfed female, likewise it can be a huge problem for a deculturated, hence, de-selfed colonized black individual. A mode and style of being that deifies the person or productions of the oppressor can be idolatrous and theologically problematical.

In an incisive probe of the psyche of a black man tortured by the reality of his blackness, Fanon caricatured the torment of a chronically conflicted black man who hated his black identity and wished it to be other than what God had created.

> Out of the blackest part of my soul, across the zebra striping of my mind surges this desire to be suddenly *white*. I wish to be acknowledged not as a *black* but as *white* now. . . . Who but a white woman can do this for me? By loving me she proves that I am worthy of white love. I am loved like a white man. I am a white man. . . . I marry white culture, white beauty, white whiteness.[74]

In this can be seen the deep psychic need and desire of the black individual to exchange the self that is for a self that is not, through sexual contact with the oppressor's female. Since the desired exchange is not biologically possible, the desire and need must remain a source of torment to the black man's psyche and a source of neurosis. And just as sexism views the female as carnal and depraved, so also racism views black skin as symbolic of subhumanity and bestiality.

> The Negro symbolizes the biological. First of all, he enters puberty at the age of nine and is a father at the age of ten; he is hot-blooded, and his blood is strong. . . . He is turned into a penis. He *is* a penis.[75]

Who would want to wear such a body, to be seen in it, and to be identified with it? It is a source of chronic self-rejection and vilification.

In *The Souls of Black Folk*, W. E. B. DuBois articulates this sense of fractured self borne by the black individual. In a timeless passage expressing the deep intrapsychic conflict of self-identity when one perceives oneself through the eyes of others, DuBois shows how a bipolar identity, or double consciousness, emerges. He argues that, among African Americans, this double consciousness is precipitated by a realization that one is both American (presumably the civilized part of one) and African (presumably the savage part), yet still rejected on both counts because even the civilized part of one is man-made, not God-made, and not quite truly human or civilized. That part reminds the oppressor of the worst in himself and is rejectable on that and other grounds. In this sense one remains a perpetual problem to oneself and to others.

> And yet, being a problem is a strange experience, peculiar even for one who has never been anything else. . . . The history of the American Negro is the history of this strife—this longing to attain self-conscious manhood, to merge his double self into a better and truer self. . . He would not bleach his Negro soul in a flood of white Amer-

icanism. . . . He simply wishes to make it possible for a man to be both a Negro and an American, without being cursed and spat upon . . . it is a peculiar sensation, this double consciousness, this sense of always looking at one's self through the eyes of others, of measuring one's soul by the tape of a world that looks on in amused contempt and pity. One ever feels his twoness—an American, a Negro; two souls, two thoughts, two unreconciled strivings; two warring ideals in one dark body, whose dogged strength alone keeps it from being torn asunder.[76]

It is possible to read DuBois's statement, "He simply wishes to make it possible for a man to be both a Negro and an American," as suggestive of a different paradigm for understanding self-identity. One such paradigm could be that of integrity-of-self. It is suggestively more relational and less individualistic than the more intrapsychic paradigms, and is truer to self. It is a more inclusive sense of self-identity in that at the same time that it experiences its own abused self, it simultaneously incorporates and includes other selves. In that way, self-identity is never unaware of other self-identities and consciously includes them. This paradigm finds its highest expression in the African sense of self-identity as explicated most notably by John Mbiti.[77]

In addition to the African view, this paradigm is supported by other non-Western perspectives on self and identity, most notably Asian, and by ethnic cultural enclaves within the United States, such as Native Americans, Puerto Ricans, Mexican Americans, and Cuban Americans.[78] In each of these family systems, the individual consciously derives her self-identity from lifetime loyalty to the extended family structure, never from personal achievement alone. The family system includes her in its consciousness of "who we are," and because she is included, her sense of who she is includes members of the family system as well. I alluded to this elastic sense of identity when earlier I defined identity as a person's sense of something called self, and an understanding of who one is in relation to that self and to significant others. I posited that identity implies a qualitative measure of one's sense of belonging in the social order, and a clarified view of the humanity with which a person feels a sense of common personhood or destiny.

Even though this view of self-identity exists in the various ethnicities within the United States, it remains doubtful that DuBois's statement is a celebration of a similar discovery within the African American community. The context does not easily lend itself to this reading of DuBois.

More pertinently, DuBois seems to be lamenting the absence of just such connectedness. DuBois sees the African American sense of self as essentially at war with itself and the world. He talks about the strife one feels at being an African American, and the longing to merge this split self into a better and truer self. DuBois expresses the wish that, lacking this integration of the two warring selves, the African American could at least "make it possible to be both Negro and an American." He ends by expressing the ultimate pain one always feels as an African American: "two souls, two thoughts, two unreconciled strivings; two warring ideals in one dark body, whose dogged strength alone keeps it from being torn asunder."

It is hard to find in this passage a celebration of a feeling of "belonging to any social order and a clarified view of the humanity with which a person feels a sense of common personhood or destiny." What emerges from DuBois's statement is a chronic feeling of rejection, an incessant need for inclusion or, failing that, a wish to be left alone. Painfully, in DuBois's thought, even that does not seem to be achievable. What is left is a sense of "always looking at one's self through the eyes of others, of measuring one's soul by the tape of the world that looks on in amused contempt and pity." If this is not the epitome of a split psyche, then it is hard to see what is. It seems very difficult for such a split psyche to feel inclusive and included in a way congruent with the African or Asian senses of self-identity.

The African sense of self-identity of which Mbiti speaks seems tied to a secure sense of one's place in the sociocultural order. It presupposes a felt sense of acceptance by the significant systems and institutions of the culture, and one's acceptance of that acceptance. Once accepted, one can accept oneself and other selves, and include them in one's integrity of being. DuBois seems to be pressing threefold truths.

The first one is that it is difficult for the African American to accept who she is because the significant culture surrounding her does not accept who she is. The second one is that it is difficult for her to accept other selves because there is no true self to accept other selves. The third truth DuBois seems to be pressing is that it is difficult for the African American to be what she chooses to be because she will not be left alone to exercise the choices available to others. She is always an issue, a question mark, a problem. She is a being at war with self and others.

Paul Tillich adds clarity to the problem DuBois addresses when he states, "No self-acceptance is possible if one is not accepted in a person-to-person relation."[79] He writes that it requires extraordinary courage even to accept acceptance, let alone rejection, and use it as an aspect of integrated self-identity. DuBois seems to be stressing the deeper problem of how to accept oneself after being unaccepted and feeling unacceptable. A coherent sense of self is nearly impossible after this wreckage. → *my childhood trauma*

Indeed, Tillich resolves the dilemma by positing a theological paradigm as a possible basis for self-identity. He locates this paradigm in "the Pauline-Lutheran doctrine of justification by faith."[80] Tillich's interpretation of this doctrine anticipates King's thinking about identity and its strides toward theological ultimacy as one basis of self-identity. DuBois did not press his analysis that far. Tillich implied it, but named it "the courage to be," or "the courage of confidence."[81]

Echoing DuBois's theme of self-estrangement from the true self is the Black Consciousness movement of South Africa. Spearheaded by the late Steve Biko, this movement sought (and still seeks) to deculturate a decultured black people and to reacculturate them so they can claim their true selves through their own eyes, not through the white eyes of the apartheid system.

The essential tenet of this movement is a simultaneous deconstruction and reconstruction of the fabricated sense of self so that the God-created self can emerge. The movement seeks to affirm one's blackness and to disaffirm one's non-whiteness. Inasmuch as nonmaleness is not a sexual category, so is nonwhiteness not a racial category, and therefore, not a basis for self-identity.

> Black Consciousness implies a vision of the heritage of our forefathers. It is the begin-
> ning of a new search for roots to anchor us firmly in the midst of a military struggle.
> It is not only a search for humanity but is an assertion and affirmation of the worth
> and dignity of the black man. . . . The real black people are those who embrace the
> positive description "black" rather than the negatives of others who set themselves up
> as the standard, the criterion and hallmark of value. It is a positive confrontation with
> the self. Black Consciousness seeks for a social content of the lives of the black people,
> and to involve the one in the suffering of the others, for this has been the cornerstone
> of the traditional black community.[82]

Identity Problems of the Underclass

In *Pedagogy of the Oppressed*, Paulo Freire offers an analysis of the identity problems facing both oppressors and the oppressed, based on class oppression. Both, he claims, suffer loss of true sense of self through the dehumanization process and the fear of freedom, albeit for different reasons.

Freire writes that dehumanization is a necessary and consequent result of oppression; that it distorts "the vocation of becoming more fully human" which is the only true human vocation.[83]

> Dehumanization, which marks not only those whose humanity has been stolen, but
> also (though in a different way) those who have stolen it is a *distortion* of the vocation
> of becoming more fully human. This distortion occurs within history; but it is not an
> historical vocation.[84]

Freire equates self-identity with one's true humanity. The oppressors' humanity is distorted due to the fact that their identity is predicated not on who they are as human beings but on the fact that they have or own things. Among the things they own are other human beings, the oppressed. However, this ownership is based not on their superior human capacities or abilities but on their perfected skill to exploit, steal, cheat, kill, rape, and plunder the oppressed. In so doing, they are alienated from their true identity, since they identify only with the negative and inhuman parts of themselves. They are unable to experience their authentic self, the human within them.

The oppressed as victims (objects) of their oppressors' conflicts (distorted subjectivity) introject and internalize the identity of the oppressor and, in the process, lose their authentic sense of self as well. They do this because they adopt an attitude of "adhesion" to the oppressor.[85]

> The very structure of their thought has been conditioned by the contradictions of the concrete, existential situation by which they are shaped. Their ideal is to be men; but for them, to be men is to be oppressors. This is their model of humanity. This phenomenon derives from the fact that the oppressed, at a certain moment of their existential experience, adopt an attitude of "adhesion" to the oppressor. Under these circumstances they cannot "consider" him sufficiently clearly to objectivize him—to discover him "outside" of themselves.[86]

By this Freire means that the oppressed objectivize the oppressor; that is, they see the oppressor as part of themselves. As a result, the oppressed see oppressors as their model of humanity, which they emulate or identify with. This behavior on the part of the oppressed is prescribed behavior; it represents an imposition of the oppressors' value system to which the oppressed conform.

Freire argues that this prescribed behavior on the part of the oppressed represents a loss of freedom because it reflects an internalization of the oppressor's image without true autonomous choice. Once this is done, further loss of freedom comes from the fear of the oppressed to liberate themselves and because of their conscious knowledge that freedom is acquired by conquest, not by gift.[87]

> One of the basic elements of the relationship between the oppressor and oppressed is prescription. Every prescription represents the imposition of one man's choice upon another, transforming the consciousness of the man transcribed to into one that conforms with the prescriber's consciousness. Thus, the behavior of the oppressed is a prescribed behavior, following as it does the guidelines of the oppressor. The oppressed, having internalized the image of the oppressor and adopted his guidelines, are fearful of freedom. Freedom would require them to eject this image and replace it with autonomy and responsibility. Freedom is acquired by conquest, not by gift. It must be pursued constantly and responsibly. Freedom is not an ideal located outside of man. ... It is rather the indispensable condition for the quest for human completion.[88]

The prospect of combat or struggle terrorizes the oppressed into complicity and submission. The result is that the oppressed are dehumanized because they are oppressed and the oppressors are dehumanized because they dehumanize the oppressed. The resultant sense of self of the oppressed is conflicted, divided, twisted, and unauthentic inasmuch as "they live in the duality in which *to be* is *to be like*, and *to be like* is to be like the oppressor."[89] Freire postulates that the identity of the oppressed turns out to be the pseudo identity of the oppressor. He prescribes a pedagogy of praxis to redeem the oppressed from this fractured sense of self through consciousness raising.

Without questioning the keen insight and razor-sharp logic Freire brings to his analysis of the psychology of powerlessness, it is possible to temper the seeming absoluteness of some of his conclusions. For instance, it is arguable that the unauthentic sense of self Freire ascribes to the oppressor may not be the total sense of self. It may exist side by side and in constant dialog with the authentic sense of self. This dialog may at times be conflicted, but it need not always lead to the distorted subjectivity Freire suggests. It could be the basis of an awareness and ownership of a multidimensional sense of self which the datum of living per se requires.

The self-identity dimension in which one might most clearly find expression would be a function of context and choice, not necessarily an ineluctable prescription rooted in a tradition of being an oppressor. However limited or constricted, the range of choices might depend on countervailing sociocultural forces. The freedom to dissent from the prescriptions of an oppressing culture is never totally denied the oppressor. Perhaps this is one way to understand the revolt of affluent youth in the 1960s against revered social institutions and the Vietnam War. Although shaped by an oppressive and imperialistic cosmology, they chose to dissent from it. Of course, the opportunity for dissent had to present itself; nevertheless, once presented, its seizure by those nurtured by the oppressing culture argues against absolutizing the loss of authentic selfhood by the oppressor.

There is another side to this suggested tempering of Freire's conclusions. It concerns the pseudo identity of the oppressed derived from the pseudo identity of the oppressor. While Freire is largely correct that, by and large, the oppressed identify with the humanhood of the oppressor, it may not follow that their own true sense of human identity is annihilated in the process. On the other hand, the correctness of Freire's insight is supported by the fact that police departments or governments headed by the previously powerless segment of society are no less brutal. For example, charges of police brutality are not uncommon against police departments headed by black chiefs of police in this country. On the nation-state level, no one seriously denies that the governments of Idi Amin and Milton Obote wreaked havoc on Ugandan people. Other black African dictatorships can be cited.

One explanation for these excesses is Freire's view that these rulers inherited and appropriated their paradigm of statecraft from their colonial masters. For them, to be a ruler is to be like the replaced colonial master—this despite the fact that in the traditional tribal cultures a ruler's primary function was to forge consensus, not to impose his will. Benevolences were earned, not exacted. African tribal cultures never

experienced the onerous taxation of Europe's feudal system, w
backbone of the American slave system and, in modified form, the
of colonized territories.

Still, as persuasive as is Freire's analysis of the adhesive identity o
it does not exhaust all analytical possibilities. One such is that, instea_ ⌄ a complete
loss of authentic self-identity, there evolves a multifaceted and multilayered way of
negotiating self-identity that accurately discerns the conflicts and pseudonymity of
the oppressor's identity and learns to effectively function within it without losing
one's own. This mode of defining one's identity takes into account the survival
requirements of the context, functionally adapts to them but still preserves the
integrity of self. This mode also lends itself to a self-identity of actual or implied solidarity among the oppressed, consonant with the definition of identity as partly a
clarified view of the humanity with which a person feels a sense of common personhood or humanity. The awareness by the oppressed of the oppressor's distorted subjectivity and their abstention from its total introjection tempers some of the abso-
lutist conclusions of Freire's otherwise acute insight and analysis.

Oppression and Self-Esteem

The descent from a fractured sense of self to diminished self-esteem is short; in fact,
the two issues are twins. That every human being needs a positive self-esteem in
order to function as an effective person is axiomatic. A preeminent psychologist,
Alfred Adler, argued that the supreme law of life is that "the sense of worth of the
self shall not be allowed to be diminished."[90] By the sense of worth of the self, Adler
meant self-esteem. When he wrote these words, Alfred Adler was keenly aware of
how powerfully social forces shaped both one's sense of self or identity and one's
self-worth or self-esteem. He believed that the latter was part of a larger problematic,
which he termed the inferiority or superiority complex, and blamed discouragement on it.

In their book *Women and Self-Esteem*, Linda Tschirhart Sanford and Mary Ellen
Donovan help clarify the distinction between self-concept and self-esteem.[91]

Self-concept or self-image is the set of beliefs and images we all have and hold to be
true of ourselves. By contrast, our level of self-esteem (or self-respect, self-love or self-
worth) is the measure of how much we like and approve of our self-concept.[92]

I use identity synonymously with self or self-concept to denote a sense of who
one believes oneself to be in relation to oneself and to significant others. Self-esteem
is, therefore, how one feels about what one believes oneself to be. In other words,
"self-esteem is the reputation you have with yourself."[93]

Sanford and Donovan also helpfully distinguish between two types of self-esteem. Global self-esteem refers to how one feels about oneself overall or as a whole. Specific self-esteem has to do with how one feels about a particular aspect or part of oneself such as, for example, one's intelligence or ability to fly an airplane. Specific self-esteem approximates self-confidence, but is not synonymous with it. For example, a black athlete may feel confident about playing some particular sport but feel awful overall about the status of being black in America.

There is a fine distinction between self-concept (the sense of oneself) and self-esteem (how one feels about oneself); and there are discernible commonalities in the way the oppressed feel about themselves, that is, the self-esteem they enjoy. A discussion of these commonalities may be heuristic.

Self-hate is one such feeling. From a belief that they are nobodies, defective or inadequate, the oppressed can hate that which they are. It is not easy to love a negative, a nobody, a nothingness. The proverbial black-on-black crime is a symptom of black self-hate. For example, in 1986, 84 percent of all violent crimes committed against blacks were committed by black offenders.[94] This phenomenon seems to stem from complex factors. In the first place, it stems from a socially imposed devaluation of the self that is deeply resented as unfair and wrong. The devaluation is experienced as carping and chronic. The oppressed acquiesce to the devaluation out of felt necessity, and the tension created by the acquiescence contributes, in a major way, to the rage they feel toward their oppressors. This is rage seeking expression and, when unexpressed, it is potentially explosive.

Nevertheless, due to an overwhelming perception of police power arrayed against them, the oppressed dare not safely strike against the true object of their rage—the oppressor. It is, therefore, turned inward and manifests itself either as reckless and irresponsible living or as criminal behavior against others.

In stark symbolism, this is implosive or self-destructive rage. Its grounding is resentment of socially imposed devaluations of the sense of self. Further, the futility experienced from an inability to deflect the devaluations transmutes the rage into self-hate and low self-esteem. These feelings are introjections of socially imposed devaluations. They reflect both a necessary acceptance of one's denigration and a sense of fraudulent participation in it.

Grier and Cobbs's *Black Rage* is a classic study of how low social evaluation of African Americans by whites has resulted in rage against the latter, and how the unexpressed rage has imploded into self-hate and low self-esteem.[95] These phenomena have, in part, deflected black rage from its true white object to the black self. Often, this is due to the fact that it is easier and safer to unleash such violence within a mostly circumscribed context where detection or apprehension is difficult. It is due also to the perception of the cheapness of black life, life which society's police power is least likely to protect or retribute. Talking about women, Sanford and Donovan state that people with low self-esteem find the world overwhelming at best and downright threatening at worst. Often, their fear and self-hatred lead to hostility toward others. . . . The talent one develops for self-hatred can easily be applied to others—especially certain groups (Jews, women, Hispanics, etc.).[96]

She might have added blacks. Anne Wilson Schaef writes that women feel relatively safer attacking other women than men, who are the real targets of resentment.[97] Paulo Freire shows how the self-hate the oppressed feel is directed against other members of the oppressed class. The oppressed themselves "become oppressors, or sub-oppressors. . . . Their ideal is to be men; but for them to be men is to be oppressors."[98] It can be seen then that self-hate, expressed in destruction of others of the same race, class, or sex, is a projective form of truncated self-esteem.

A pervasive feeling of powerlessness is another generic manifestation of low or diminished self-esteem. This is a feeling of immobility, hopelessness, and grief; a feeling of not being in control of one's own body or one's destiny, and an impotence to do something about it. According to Grier and Cobbs, grief and sorrow have been the overriding experience of African Americans in the United States.[99]

In *Therapy with Women*, Susan Sturdivant lists six types of power differentials between men and women: normative power (sex-role based); institutional power (access to money, education, and influence); reward power (reward the compliant only); expertise power (pervasive male expertise); psychological power (institutional-fit presumption); and power of brute force (rape, physical violence).[100]

Even though this typology is meant to describe the male-female matrix only, it applies to racially based and class-based oppression as well. This is because oppression is a consequence of the usurpation of power by the oppressor and denial of same to the oppressed. Powerless people feel a sense of diminished self-esteem that shows itself in symptoms such as depression.

Anne Wilson Schaef has succinctly summarized the relative power differential between men and women in this manner:

> There is something men have that we (women) would very much like to have . . . the birthright of innate superiority, the *power* and influence one inherits by being born male. A man can be less competent or knowledgeable than a woman, but he still has the advantage over her simply because he is a man. It really does not matter whether or not men consciously know that they have this birthright. Most assume it at a very basic level. Women know it and this awareness affects the way we see ourselves, men and other women.[101]

But for the fact that Anne Schaef is writing about how women feel about men, the same could be said of how the racially nonwhite feel about white people and how the underclass feels about the middle and upperclass. The power matrix shapes and characterizes the relationships. And when the underclass also happen to be women of color, then Anne Schaef's statement has a triple sting in that the oppressive forces of classism, sexism, and racism converge to impose themselves.

It is apparent, however, that there is an overarching ideology over and above all these ideologies—that of power. For instance, while male domination may explain the oppression of women, it fails to explain the oppression of racial minorities and the underclass. Equally true is the fact that women themselves have oppressed other women, other races, and the underclasses. Note can be taken of the fact that British imperialism peaked when Victoria was queen. Trade in slaves became institutionalized when Elizabeth I was queen of England. British Prime Minister Margaret Thatcher exhibited intransigent opposition to black rule in South Africa.

Power—its acquisition, wielding, and abuse—seems to be the ideology behind the ideologies. The other ideologies subserve the ideology of power. This might explain why the oppressed collude in their own oppression to their continuing detriment; power can be subtle and seductive. That its abuse can dehumanize the oppressed and oppressors alike is very instructive.

TWO

___

KING'S PERSPECTIVE ON IDENTITY FORMATION
AND ITS PROBLEMS

Identity is a lifelong vocation. It is a ceaseless process. We rework our identities as we traverse the seasons of life. It is also intimately inter-relational and communal. There is an aspect of us in each significant past and present relationship and experience. The tapestry of life contributes to our respective identities.

Even though King was not a professionally trained psychologist, he had keen psychological insights concerning the psychological problems of identity, self-esteem, and powerlessness experienced by the oppressed. This chapter presents King's constructive thought on the problems of identity as experienced by the oppressed. King does not embrace any particular school of psychology or systematically expound any particular psychological perspective. He seems, however, well-acquainted with aspects of varied personality theories, which he employs in his vocation as a practical theologian. His use of psychological insights betrays a familiarity with both psychodynamic theories and social-psychological perspectives on personality. He deftly integrates these with his theological intuitions to envision a usable perspective on identity that is simultaneously philosophical, sociotheological, and psychodynamic. While the focus of his thinking is the condition of the African American, the crucible of his thought has applicability to other oppressed communities or groups.

King's views on identity expose a deep conviction concerning its philosophical grounding:

The Negro will only be truly free when he reaches down to the inner depths of his own being and signs with the pen and ink of assertive selfhood his own emancipation proclamation. With a spirit straining toward true self-esteem, the Negro must throw off the manacles of self-abnegation and say to himself and the world: "I am somebody. I am a person. I am a man with dignity and honor."[1]

Two interrelated themes are evident in this passage: one addresses the issue of self-esteem discussed in the next chapter; the other addresses the issue of identity presently before us.

Throughout his writings and speeches, King makes clear that, at a philosophical level, the human is a metaphysical being. That is, the human is not a derivative being. He or she simply is. For King, the personhood of man or woman is not conferred by any other human person. The "beingness" or "I-amness" of a person does not derive from other human beings or from social institutions that are consequences and repositories of culture. This is the ontological basis of identity that King consistently asserts and emphasizes: I am a person, I am somebody, whether or not someone else thinks so and acknowledges me to be so.

King's views concerning the ontological basis of identity contrast with those of Erik Erikson, whose perspective is rooted in biological epigenesis, which describes simultaneously a process of biological maturation, identity formation, and the broader aspects of personality change. For Erikson, identity formation is intensely thematized around the adolescent period. King's views also contrast with those of Robert Kegan, whose notion of identity is the evolutionary motion or process itself. For Kegan, identity is the "how" of how the self becomes other, not the otherness itself. Both these perspectives suggest an evolutionary basis for understanding identity, not an ontological one. That is, they suggest a "becomingness," not a "beingness" of identity. King's philosophical position of identity asserts the latter.

The significance of King's conception of identity as philosophically ontological is fourfold. First, it allows King to argue that identity is prior to culture; therefore it is immoral for institutions and their safeguarders to abuse the powerless or nonwhite on grounds that they are nobodies. No human being is a nobody. Second, it allows King to urge the dispossessed to claim the true selves robbed of them by culture. Third, it allows King to rebuke society and its leaders for presiding over institutions and laws that fracture and disturb the selves of the oppressed. Fourth, it allows King to diagnose the psychological problems of the oppressed as etiologically rooted not in genetic inferiority, but in their dehumanization. In taking this stance, King's views are in accord with those of feminist, ethnic, and non-Western thinkers concerning the link between mental health and oppression and suffering.

In postulating an ontology of identity formation, King is also in league with a preeminent "personologist," Alfred Adler.[2] Adler postulated that, at birth, human beings are endowed with a prepotent dynamic force, which he variously named "will to power," "compensatory action," "masculine protest," and "striving for superiority." Even though this innate, dynamic force had a biological dimension and unfolded in culture, it was deeper than biology and ontologically prior to culture. It was, in King's vocabulary, innate and inherent personhood or somebodiness. For Adler, it was this innate prepotency that shapes and fuels human identity formation and which, if frustrated by culture, results in pathology. For Adler, discouragement is the major sociocultural trigger of pathology.[3]

Echoing King and Adler in their ontology of human identity are Paulo Freire—who terms identity "authentic self" or "true human vocation"—and the Black Consciousness movement of South Africa, which decries the loss of self-affirmed and self-defined identity due to the ravages of the apartheid system.[4]

King's Sociotheological Basis for Identity

Even stronger than his conviction that the human being is an ontological somebody is King's conviction that every person is socially embedded and theologically endowed and derives identity ultimately from the Judeo-Christian God. For King, these two realities converge to decisively shape identity formation. Thus, when King exhorts his black audience to assert their somebodiness and personhood, he is simultaneously urging them to claim their socially and divinely derived selves and is confirming and conferring upon them these bases for identity.

King views human identity as inextricably tied to human society; for him, this means human relationships and institutions. Further, it means global human relationships and institutions. It is a central tenet of King's thought and belief system that human identity is inconceivable without this global human and relational web. This inextricable social and human relatedness gives the human person an additional basis for the "I-amness" and "I-am-somebodiness" ontology discussed earlier.

Importantly, this basis for self-identity is not exclusively an interiorized, intrapsychic consciousness of the self. It is a social confirmation of one's place in the social order. It is an identity wrought simultaneously by an ontological claim to selfhood and a demand that society acknowledge this claim. King posits that one's membership in human sociality·ineluctably confers identity upon one.

While King is acquainted with intrapsychic theories that seek to explain human psychopathology, he does not seem to hold their intrapsychic explication of psychopathology as decisive.[5] He argues that environmental forces are decisive shapers of both identity and psychopathology.[6]

On the question of the environmental basis for human identity, King is emphatic that social embeddedness is the key factor:

> The next truth is evidential in the history of mankind. Not only are all men alike . . .
> but man is by nature a societal creature. . . . The universe is so structured that things
> do not quite work out rightly if men are not diligent in their concern for others. The
> self cannot be self without other selves. It cannot reach fulfillment without thou.
> Social psychologists tell us that we cannot truly be persons unless we interact with
> other persons. All life is interrelated. All men are caught in an inescapable network of
> mutuality, tied in a single garment of destiny.[7]

This view that social embeddedness decisively shapes human identity has three consequences for King. First, it shapes his view of human pathology as socially derived and as mirroring prevailing social pathology. Second, it informs his belief that alleviation of human pathology lies in the transformation or elimination of distress-causing social forces. Third, it allows him to believe that social groups can suffer group pathology, a perspective lacking in the intrapsychic orientations of both Erikson and Kegan. While Kegan acknowledges the formative and disabling aspects of the embeddedness culture, unlike King he is silent on corporate or group pathology. For instance, King views segregation as social leprosy and sees blacks as the principal and major symptom bearers of this leprosy. He bemoans both the physical and psychological symptoms of this leprosy:

> This is why segregation has wreaked havoc with the Negro. It is sometimes difficult to determine which are the deepest wounds, the physical or the psychological. Only a Negro can understand the social leprosy that segregation inflicts upon him. Like a nagging ailment, it follows his every activity, leaving him tormented by day and haunted by night. The suppressed fears and resentments, and the expressed anxieties and sensitivities make each day a life of turmoil. Every confrontation with the restrictions against him is another emotional battle in a never-ending war.[8]

A cursory reading of the above statement might leave one with the impression that King is merely describing external restrictions on a black person similar to external restrictions on other types of people. Such is not the case. A correct interpretation of King's thought must acknowledge that King has a deeply felt conviction that social restrictions against a black person go beyond the ordinary. His use of "social leprosy" to describe these restrictions discloses the true meaning of King's conviction. He is aware of the restrictions against the Jews and decries them; likewise against the poor in general, and against Southern poor in particular. He is enraged by the ravages of the Vietnam War against the Vietnamese. In none of these contexts does King employ "social leprosy" to describe the felt anguish of the affected.

Inherent in his use of this symbolic expression is a sense of deep psychic trauma symptomized by torment, phobias, paranoia, anxiety, rage, and emotional turmoil. Shame and dread are clearly implied in these symptoms in that leprosy is a shameful and dreadful disease. It is public in its social manifestation, but equally private in its emotional and psychological wreckage. King is depicting a leprosy not only of the skin (the external restrictions suffered by many others), but also of the psyche— the latter suffered only by a Negro. "Only a Negro can understand the social leprosy that segregation inflicts upon him. Like a nagging ailment, it follows his every activity, leaving him tormented by day and haunted by night."

The quoted statement depicts a sense of self chronically tortured and almost never integrated. It is most unlikely that a chronically phobic, paranoid, anxious, and enraged person can achieve an integrated sense of self. The restrictions King notes seem to refer specifically to those engendered by segregation itself, not nebulous or ordinary types. King symbolizes segregation as "social leprosy" to impress on society its uniquely debilitating nature, and to stress that in the United States black persons are the only social beings who bear this type of social badge. Thus, the key insight expressed in this passage is that the psychic trauma that fractures the sense of self of a black person reflects fracturing forces inherent in the society in which the self is embedded. Groups are "selves" that can suffer fracture as well. For King, blacks in America are such a group on which segregation wreaks group psychic havoc.

In offering this insight on the effect of the environment on identity formation, King is at one with the "underside psychologists" such as, for example, the feminists, Freire, DuBois, Fanon, Grier and Cobbs, and the Black Consciousness advocates of South Africa. These and similar ethnic thinkers likewise regard sociocultural forces as decisive in shaping and disabling human identity.

Theological Ultimacy as Ultimate Basis for Identity in King's Thought

In King's thought, one's somebodiness, in addition to being ontologically and socially embedded, has theological ultimacy. That is, its undisputed anchor is that a person is God's creature and part of God's personality. For King, this is decisive for one's identity and value. In this chapter focus is on identity. The issue of value or worth is considered in the next chapter.

King does not conceive of a human identity that is not simultaneously etched in, and derived from, God's own. God bestows identity as part of God's own image and confers value on it by reason of divine creation alone. To make this point, King says this:

> Deeply rooted in our religious heritage is the conviction that every man is an heir to a legacy of dignity and worth. Our Judeo-Christian tradition refers to inherent dignity of man in the Biblical term 'the image of God'. . . . Every human being has etched in his personality the indelible stamp of the creator. . . . The worth of the individual does not lie in the measure of his intellect, his racial origin or his social position. Human worth lies in relatedness to God. An individual has value because he has value to God.[9]

Three themes emerge here. First, an individual has value because God confers it on her. God confers value on the human because God has value. This can be viewed as King's value theory, ultimately substantiated by Christian faith and theology. Second, an individual has identity because she is created in God's image, is related to God and embodies God's personality. Third, and by implication, treatment of humans on the basis of their social evaluation is an "objectification" of them and a distortion of their true, God-derived identity.

King sees segregation as a major culprit in the destruction of human identity formed in God's image. Segregation objectifies persons and desecrates them. This desecration is the ultimate fracturing of human identity, in that it abuses God's personality as well. The desecration occurs to the oppressor as well as the oppressed. On this issue King says this:

> But man is not a thing. He must be dealt with not as an "animated tool" but as a person sacred in himself. To do otherwise is to depersonalize the potential person and desecrate what he is. So long as the Negro or any other member of a minority group is treated as a means to an end, the image of God is abused in him and consequently and proportionately lost by those who inflict the abuse.[10]

This is a remarkable insight on King's part. It is both simply commonsensical and deeply theological. It is a matter of common sense that each time a child is molested or otherwise abused the parents are likewise deeply affected and derivatively feel the child's pain and anguish. Also, oftentimes it is the caregivers who feel greater excruciating emotional and spiritual agony than the comatose patient. God as the ultimate parent suffers gravely each time God's own child is abused. It is also a matter of common sense that in order to put and keep someone down, you too have to be down there with him. You have to keep watch. You have to expend material and spiritual resources to keep guard. In the process your own personality and humanity is retarded and warped. For example, the personalities of many dictators are limited and warped by the extent to which they expend their energies and resources to keep their subjects in their places. In the United States, the economies of states of the Deep South stagnated by the degree to which over decades these police states expended resources to put the African American down and keep him there. Unfortunately, both the European American and the African American suffered from economic stagnation in comparison to other regions of the country. The hostility, meanness, and crudeness required to keep any humanity in its place shows up in the absence of social and cultural achievements of a whole nation or region. The basest of instincts are required to perpetrate such a wrong or evil, and these instincts can infuse a whole culture or personality. Clearly, God cannot and does not bless or celebrate the abuse of God's own creatures. By abusing other creatures the abuser commits sin against the majesty of God's throne of cosmic justice and righteousness. The blood of the abused cries in heaven in search of God's justice and righteousness. The Judgment Day pericope of Matthew 25:31–46 is a stirring illustration of this theological truth. So also is the Cain and Abel story of Genesis 4:8–12. King's thought embraces both truths.

King's Theological Perspective on Identity Formation in
Conversation with James Fowler

———

James Fowler is a theologian and structural developmental psychologist who has done seminal work on faith as a human vocation. He has conducted research and written extensively on faith development theory; he presents faith as a human activity that develops through stages ranging from "primal" to "universalizing."[11]

Fowler writes as a social scientist acknowledging indebtedness to constructive cognitive developmentalists such as Jean Piaget and Lawrence Kohlberg, and to the psychosocial ego developmentalist Erik H. Erikson.[12] He writes as a theologian indebted to Paul Tillich and H. Richard Niebuhr, particularly the latter.[13] Fowler is neither a historian of religion nor a scholar of comparative religion, but he has relied significantly on the intuitions of Wilfred Cantwell Smith, who is such, in distinguishing between faith and religion or belief.[14]

Fowler also writes as a structuralist in the sense that in depicting the developmental stages of faith he is not so much concerned about the content or "whatness" of faith as about how faith develops. Fowler's faith development theory attends to the structures that shape the person's "faithing" enterprise; that is, the theory concerns itself with how the person relates to self, others, and God; how she constructs meaning out of these relationships; and how ultimately she shapes her life's projects as a consequence of these relationships and the meanings she makes of them. Since this activity is both social and theological, Fowler's faith development theory is a rich, integrated model of psychological and theological development throughout the life span.

Fowler's project has importance for this book because of its contribution to the study of identity formation as understood by King. It was shown above how, for King, identity formation as an expression of one's somebodiness has theological ultimacy. This writer believes that, even though it is not generally acknowledged, Fowler's faith development theory, instead of being understood vaguely as a study of the "central dynamic in human development,"[15] can be studied as a seminal contribution to an understanding of identity formation as King theologically conceives of it. This writer proposes that the "central dynamic in human development" ascribed to Fowler's theory and project is identity formation as understood by King. King's conception of identity derives its ultimate image and value from God; so, evidently, does Fowler's. No other writer has interpreted Fowler's theory in this manner; what is being pressed here is a novel interpretation and use of Fowler. To crystallize this conversation between King's conception of identity and that of Fowler as reflected in his faith development theory, Fowler's view of faith is briefly examined.

While it has received reformulations and refinements, Fowler's definition of faith in *Stages of Faith* illuminates how identity formation is a central thrust of his theory. For Fowler, faith is:

> People's evolved and evolving ways of experiencing self, others and world (as they construe them) as related to and affected by the ultimate conditions of existence (as they construct them) and of shaping their lives' purposes and meanings, trusts and loyalties, in light of the character of being, value and power determining the ultimate conditions of existence (as grasped in their operative images—conscious and unconscious—of them).[16]

From this definition three themes can be identified. The first is that faith is relational; it is the human vocation of relating to self, others, and the community as one composes these realities to be. Implicit in this relationality is the interpersonality of faith. Faith is both relational and interpersonal. Fowler makes this aspect of faith explicit when he states:

> Faith begins in relationship. Faith implies trust in another, reliance upon another, counting upon or dependence upon another. The other side of faith as trust is faith as attachment, as commitment, as loyalty.[17]

This is the covenantal dimension of faith.

The second theme is that faith is one way of knowing and valuing. It is one way of construing, comprehending, perceiving, seeing, noticing, and understanding life, the world, and the people in it and of placing value or worth on what is known. This is the meaning-making function of faith in which self-worth and self-identity are at stake as well. Fowler calls this process "constitutive-knowing"[18] and distinguishes two types of logic in its quest: the logic of rational certainty and that of conviction.[19] The former logic is the cognitive and scientific mode of knowing; the latter is the affective and passional. Thus faith as a dimension of knowing is both rational and intellectual as well as emotional and imaginative. Fowler confirms this facet of knowing in this statement:

> Faith shapes its initiatives and responses in our lives on the basis of modes of knowing which combine imagination, valuing, or affections and reasoning in a complex "logic of conviction." The symbols, rituals, stories and teaching of religious traditions as well as other ideological systems can become the mundane causes of faith's awakening and growth.[20]

The third theme arising from Fowler's definition of faith is that it is a triadic structure. The "faithing" vocation is not only interrelational and interpersonal, it is also triangular: it shapes and deepens life projects by connecting and rooting them in ultimate centers of value and power. For Fowler this is the pinnacle of meaning making as a "faithing" vocation: the construction of life projects that commit the self to an ultimate environment.

> This is that most inclusive triangle in which the self relates to the canvas of making of meaning itself. . . . I have referred to this largest canvas of meaning as our sense of an *ultimate environment*. In Jewish and Christian terms, the ultimate environment is expressed with the symbol "Kingdom of God." In this way of seeing, *God* is the center of power and value which unifies and gives character to the ultimate environment.[21]

For Fowler, therefore, faith is a way of being in relation to self, to other selves, and to centers of value and power—of which the ultimate is God. This self engages in reflective and covenantal activity that includes perspective taking. Meaning is made and remade as the self traverses the life span and appropriates the community's symbols, rituals, and master stories and identifies with them. This is a constant reworking of self-identity, where confirmation, valuation, and transformation derive ultimately from membership in the commonwealth of the creator, governor, and redeemer God.

It was shown earlier that, for King, personal identity derives ultimately from the personality of the Creator,[22] who shapes it by the act of creation and by eternal relationship with the creature. It was also shown that, for King, personal and human value derives from the same source because the source has inherent value. It was further demonstrated that, for King, identity devolves from the ontology of being, as well as from social embeddedness. Fowler echoes this sense when he talks about faith as a way of being in relation to self (ontology), to other selves (sociality), and to centers of value and power.[23]

King's ontological grounding of identity interfaces with Fowler's ontological view of faith when the latter asserts that "different faiths are alternate modes of being in the world that arise out of contrasting ways of composing the ultimate conditions of existence. Ways of being and ways of seeing are reciprocal."[24] Fowler does not use the term "faith" in the exclusively religious sense. To the contrary, his faith development theory disavows this narrow understanding of this rich phenomenon. While faith may include religious faith, it need not do so. Fowler's focus is on faith as a universal human vocation of being, seeing, knowing, valuing, relating, composing, construing, and becoming; in short, the defining and reworking of one's identity in the journey through life.

King's Perspective on Identity in Contrast with
Those of Erikson and Kegan

In order to achieve optimal clarity, King's psychological insights on the issue of identity and its challenges are now contrasted with the ego psychoanalytic perspective of Erik H. Erikson and the constructive developmental perspective of Robert Kegan, both well-known masters of personality theory. The chapter will conclude by suggesting potential contributions of King's constructive thought to work with individuals from oppressed groups presenting identity problems.

Erikson's perspective on identity formation is psychosocial in orientation and heavily indebted to Freud's psychoanalytic theory. However, unlike Freud, whose interest was in treating hysteria and neurosis in middle-class Viennese women, Erikson's preoccupation is with identity formation in youth, particularly adolescents.[25] His psychosocial developmental stages mirror Freud's psychosexual stages through Freud's genital stage, which is Erikson's adolescence.[26] Erikson employs Freudian psychosexual, biological principles, and Freud's intrapsychic conflictual psychology to account for identity formation. He retains the Freudian stage concept of human development, and introduces the object-relations concept of object incorporation to explicate identity formation through adolescence. He employs the insights of contemporary ego psychology to account for personality development beyond adolescence to the entire life span, and to account for the impact of sociocultural forces on biology.[27] He introduces object relations into the theory to account for the ego's interrelationality and sociality, thereby mitigating some of the harsh prescriptions of Freudian epigenetic and intrapsychic determinism.

The result is a theory of identity that remains principally chronological and intrapsychic; one that is centered on Freud's id concept through adolescence and on the superego concept thereafter, with the ego concept as the eternal regulator between the childhood id and the adulthood superego. The theory has a built-in bipolar "me" emphasis of early childhood incorporations, introjections, and identifications, and the "us" emphasis of adulthood sociality.

However, the theory does not quite succeed in clarifying what is meant by identity. One can read Erikson's theory as the unfolding of the egotistical "I" and its transformation into a social "we" after adolescence. It can also be read to mean the emergence of the Freudian superego from the id, or as the development of the ego from a primitive into a more complex structure. Erikson's theory can further be understood as the inexorable shedding of childhood object-relations introjections and identifications and their replacement by a more exteriorized sense of self. Each of these possible readings of Erikson is fraught with difficulties.

For example, if ego development is the intended meaning, confusion is introduced by the fact that the Freudian ego concept Erikson appropriated and employed is a highly nebulous intrapsychic structure that functions primarily to defend against intrapsychic anxiety. It is not quite clear how this defensive structure develops and shapes human identity. Secondly, even though the theory engages culture as an aspect of identity formation, it is not clear if culture is invoked to explain how human development occurs or how socialization occurs, and if the two are synonymous. While Erikson acknowledges the significance of religion in the formation of trustful relationships between and among persons in society,[28] his theory of identity formation is not moored in any clearly defined theological project. Nor is the role of emotions explicated in Erikson's concept of identity, which is intrapsychic, largely cognitive, and egotistical. A usable theory of identity for working with persons from oppressed groups must adequately account for the social biography of its members as a group, including its psychological dynamics, emotional tone, and religious experience.[29]

Robert Kegan is a modern developmental psychologist who views identity as a dynamic process of meaning making. Unlike Erikson, who thematizes identity around the fifth era of life-span development, Kegan postulates a life long evolutionary process of meaning making or identity formation.

In his seminal text *The Evolving Self,* Kegan draws on Erikson's ego psychoanalytic psychology, Fairburn and Winnicott's object relations, and the cognitive developmental approaches of Piaget and Kohlberg in explicating his theory of identity—which he terms constructive-developmental.[30] By this theory, Kegan seeks to explain how the sense of self evolves over the life span. He equates sense of self with self-sufficiency and self-ownership, and both, in turn, with identity.[31] For him, identity is synonymous with meaning making.

From cognitive developmental theories of Piaget and Kohlberg, Kegan appropriates the notion of·development as a construction and reconstruction of meaning. From the object-relations theories of Fairburn and Winnicott, Kegan appropriates the concept of self and object. But he uses the concepts of development and self-object in unique and creative ways in expounding his theory. For Kegan, the self is synonymous with subject and is an intrapsychic structure in which a person is so embedded that she cannot distance herself from it. The self as an intrapsychic structure changes with developmental stages. One's self is one's sensations and reflexes at age 0 and one's impulses and perceptions at age 2. One is so embedded in the intrapsychic structure that shapes one's self at any particular stage that one is not aware of one's embeddedness.

For Kegan, object does not mean the same thing it means in object-relations theory, that is, it is not an internalized image or representation of a significant other person shaping one's present behavior. It means a self from which one has succeeded in creating a distance. It means a framework from which one has disengaged and on which one can reflect. Object is that part of the self-subject that has been thrown away and that the new subjectivity has objectified, and can observe and manipulate.

> Emergence from embeddedness involves a kind of repudiation, an evolutionary re-
> cognition that what before was me is not me. . . . I started by discussing how "object
> treating" must mean "subject losing"; I have come around to showing how "subject
> losing" can lead to "object finding." This is a rhythm central to the underlying motion
> of personality.[32]

Thus, for Kegan, identity or meaning making concerns how one "throws away" that which was once a part of the self and makes it an object of a restructured self; accordingly, what one once was (subject) one now has (object). It is one's achieved ability to bring to awareness about oneself that which one was not aware of before. Kegan uses terms such as "sense of self," "self-dependence," and "self-ownership" to refer to the same phenomenon of meaning making or identity formation.[33] In turn, this phenomenon is equated with personality.[34] The awareness evolves over time and in stages that Kegan calls "truces."

Kegan's is a highly fluid and processive notion of identity. It contrasts sharply with that of other developmentalists in that it locates identity not at an achieved stage, but in the motion between stages. For Kegan, stages are only "evolutionary truces [that] establish a balance between subject and object."[35] Truces are temporary periods when the world "makes sense," but are gauges of neither personality nor identity. Development is the systematic way in which a person's boundaries between self and other change, how the subject is thrown away or objectified and how that which is thrown away is restructured into a new self or subjectivity.

> I suggest that human development involves a succession of renegotiated balances, or
> "biologies," which come to organize the experience of the individual in qualitatively
> different ways. In this sense, evolutionary activity is intrinsically cognitive, but it is no
> less affective; we are this activity and we experience it. . . . In identifying evolutionary
> activity as the fundamental ground of personality, I am suggesting that the source of
> our emotions is the phenomenological experience of evolving—of defending, surren-
> dering, and reconstructing a center.[36]

Thus, Kegan's constructive-development process has both cognition and affect. The activity gives rise to structures that define the boundaries between subject (self) and object (other). Identity or meaning making is a process in which boundaries between self and other become structured, lost, and restructured. It is the process of how a person makes sense of the world, not what sense she makes. It is the process by which the data of life are experienced, organized, and apprehended—not what is experienced, organized, and apprehended.

It can be seen that Kegan's notion of identity is an interiorized process of self-consciousness. It is highly intrapsychic: the structure or framework undergoing perpetual reconstruction is intrapsychic. It is dynamic, motional, processive, decidedly not static. It is simultaneously cognitive and affective.

Despite its intrapsychic rootedness, Kegan's identity formation or meaning making does not occur in a cultural vacuum. Kegan postulates a "holding environment" or "culture of embeddedness" that, during each evolutionary motion and truce, performs three functions essential for identity: "holding on," "letting go," and "remaining in place."[37]

One is struck by the fluidity and, at times, nebulousness of Kegan's theory. Identity as the inexorable process of meaning making makes it difficult to locate and measure the point at which identity can be said to have been achieved. Evolutionary truces are not that point because they are mere times when the world makes sense, not necessarily when one makes sense to oneself or to others. They are not even points when one achieves self-ownership, self-sufficiency, or self-competence. The truces achieve self/other or subject/object balances; it is, however, not clear if these balances are the same as identity or some other entity. Kegan suggests that identity is not these balances but the evolutionary motion itself that leads to these balances. In the same vein, this motion seems to be the measure of personality itself, which Kegan calls "person;" the evolutionary balances are what he calls "individual."[38] It is not entirely clear, therefore, whether the evolutionary motion that is identity is also personality, and whether the two are identical. It appears that they are.

Kegan's identity theory also comes across as a theory about an evolving or developing self-consciousness. The view of the person as being so embedded in one's intrapsychic framework as to be unable to create distance from it sounds perilously close to unconscious self-centration. In this state, one is one's evolutionary motion and embedded in it. This is the person's identity and, presumably, personality. The attainment of an evolutionary truce, following decentration from intrapsychic self-embeddedness, is not the attainment of identity but of subject/object balance, a distancing from the self. This suggests that in Kegan's theory one's identity is attained when one is unconscious of it—a rather troublesome notion. It suggests a deeply interiorized and introspective sense of self, uninformed and unaffected by one's sense of one's place in the created order.

Kegan seeks to correct this reading of his theory by explicitly asserting the contrary, and by proposing a "holding environment" or "culture of embeddedness" other than a person's own intrapsychic framework in which one's sense of self or subject inescapably embeds. It is not obvious that the inclusion of the holding environments in the theory purges it of its apparent aversion to culture as a shaper of identity. Kegan's holding environments seem to facilitate the intrapsychic awareness of the self/other (subject/object) distinction, but not necessarily awareness of one's ensconcement in culture as part of one's personal identity.

It is helpful to note that Erikson's theory overall is an attempt to describe personality development as the successive resolution of crises throughout the life span. For him, the crisis of identity is a reasonably circumscribed event of late adolescence that can be viewed either as a culmination of earlier *id*-centered development or as the onset of later *superego* developmental elan. Both the intrapsychic forces of Freudian psychosexual dynamics and the introjections of object-relations theory play major roles in shaping Erikson's theory of identity formation.

While the factor of culture is ambiguous in Erikson's theory, it is not so in Kegan's constructive-developmental scheme. Cultures of embeddedness are at the center of his theorizing; these subserve the functions of holding on, letting go, and remaining available as the self evolves. Further, it has been noted that the question is unresolved whether the cultures of embeddedness decisively shape the evolving sense of self, or these cultures merely provide environments in which some undefined and unnamed intrapsychic structure of personality is nurtured into self-identity. Also, it was noted that this self-identification occurs as a processive event and is apprehended effectively after self-objectification. Kegan's theory does not urge that the holding environments actively aid the reflective and self-objectification process, only that they provide a milieu in which this process unfolds. What unfolds and how it unfolds seems to be confined to the intrapsychic domain.

In dialog with both Erikson and Kegan, King's view of self-identity is decisively ontological, sociological, and theological. It is measurably liberated from the intrapsychic moorings of the other two. While informed by an ontological doctrine of man, it derives its ultimacy from a theological understanding of human self-identity. In this aspect, King's theory seems to converse fruitfully with Fowler's, whose understanding of human development as triadic meaning making also has theological ultimacy. It has been proposed that even though Fowler's has been presented and received as a faith development theory, the meaning making he proposes can be understood as reworkings of self-identities throughout the life span.

keenly felt by them. His sufferings were familiar and very personal because enslavement was no less horrific. That explained why they could sing with compassion and can still sing with sorrow, "Were you there when they crucified my Lord? Sometimes it causes me to tremble, tremble, tremble." Jesus' suffering on the cross was personally felt and continues to be personally felt by the African American suffering community.

Inasmuch as Jesus' passion represented insufferable humiliation with which the slaves could personally identify, so also was the promise and hope of the Resurrection. Jesus conquered death and was raised from the dead. Actually and symbolically the slaves too would be raised up. In God's own time, the slaves would be raised from death and join Jesus in heaven where sorrow, pain, and suffering would be no more. Death, therefore, would not have the final word. Its sting would not be eternal.

All God's children would present themselves before God's majesty, where their brother and friend Jesus was awaiting them. Before then, however, there was also the real possibility of spiritual resurrection and triumph here on earth. Through escape or sheer effort of will, the enslaving system would not fully triumph. God in Christ would see to it that the shackles of the slave system were broken, annihilated, and vanquished. Drawing the parallel between Egyptian and American bondage, Pharaoh's armies in America would also be defeated. The slaves would be physically liberated. Barring this, their spirits would triumph over the most evil system ever devised by man. So either the body would be raised up for heaven or the downcast spirits would be resurrected above the limitations of a diabolic system. Jesus' resurrection foreordained both outcomes.

King's insight that a de-selfed and tortured self-concept leads to a tormented emotional and psychic life and diminished self-esteem is supported by feminist psychologists and by Fanon and Freire, discussed earlier in this book.

Inferiority Complex in King's Thought

Coined and popularized by Alfred Adler, the term "inferiority feelings" refers to a psychological state characterized by feelings of weakness, inadequacy, and frustration. Adler theorizes that in its extreme form this feeling results in shriveled self-esteem and incapacitated psychological and emotional functioning. In that form the feeling becomes complex and pathological. He cites extreme discouragement as the chief trigger of inferiority complex. Adler believes that, in their mild form, inferiority feelings can spur growthful change and superior individual achievements.

> Inferiority feelings are not in themselves abnormal. They are the cause of all improvements in the position of mankind. . . . Indeed, it seems that all our human culture is based upon feelings of inferiority.[9]

For Adler, the overcoming of paralyzing feelings of inferiority depends on a person's taking compensatory action or striving for superiority.[10] This enhances or safeguards one's self-esteem. By compensatory action Adler simply means gaining power to overcome the felt inferiority or the diminished self-esteem. The will to power fuels one to take such action. Unfortunately, this can be power over or against others—and can be destructive of self and others unless tempered by concern for others.

A hybrid of compensatory action that Adler calls "striving for superiority" is preferable. It allows a person to develop a lifestyle and life goal aimed at acquiring power with and for others. This strategy recognizes the deep human need for love, togetherness, and cooperation. Adler names this need "social feeling," "social interest," or "community feeling."[11] For Adler, "social feeling" and "community feeling" have specific meanings. He uses these terms to describe what he understands as a need shared by all persons for "the sense of human solidarity, the connectedness of man to man in a cosmic relationship . . . the wider connotation of a 'sense of fellowship in the human community.'"[12] He understands the self not as a structure embedded somewhere in the psyche but as a dynamic principle of constant interaction with one's environment. Achievements in work, friendships, and love shape both one's sense of the self and one's self-worth. Failure in work (seen as a contribution to one's community), friendship (as a safe and secure sense of belonging in the human race), and love (as a union of mind and body) fracture one's sense of self and diminish one's self-worth. Adler regards as axiomatic the notion that "the sense of worth of the self shall not be allowed to be diminished"[13] and believes that "the feeling of personal worth can only be derived from achievement, from the ability to overcome."[14]

There are several points of contact between Adler's views on inferiority feelings and inferiority complex—and how these phenomena contribute to low self-esteem—and King's views. Adler holds that social factors and arrangements are the major culprits, as does King. For both thinkers, political, economic, and cultural arrangements are the principal causative factors. King points to the history of enslavement, slavery, and segregation as the diabolic social force.

> Throughout the era of slavery the Negro was treated in inhuman fashion. He was considered a thing to be used, not a person to be respected. He was merely a depersonalized cog in a vast plantation machine . . . living under these conditions, many Negroes lost faith in themselves. They came to feel that they were less than human.[15]

King believes that the historical black experience in America makes blacks collectively feel inferior and causes them to develop inferiority complexes as individuals. There may be individual exceptions, but these are few and rare, and the exceptions do not impeach his theory of corporate emotional and psychic devastation. It is experienced early in life as a "color shock" and endures throughout life.

Being a Negro in America means not only living with the consequences of a past of slavery and family disorganization but facing this very day the pangs of "color shock." Because the society, with unmitigated cruelty, has made the Negro's color anathema, every Negro child suffers a traumatic emotional burden when he encounters the reality of his black skin. . . . Every Negro comes face to face with this color shock, and it constitutes a major emotional crisis. It is accompanied by a sort of fatiguing, wearisome hopelessness.[16]

The traumatic emotional burden to which King refers is the inferior feeling cited by Adler, which Adler believes can serve as a springboard for ameliorative action for self and others. So does King. He states, "I do not mean to suggest that we should seek to eliminate fear altogether from human life. . . . Fear . . . is a powerfully creative force. Every great invention and intellectual advance represents a desire to escape from some dreaded circumstance or condition."[17]

Yet, like Adler, King also acknowledges that some negative social forces are so severe as to be emotionally ruinous and psychologically destructive.[18] He calls these debilitating fears abnormal. In making this distinction, King joins Adler in distinguishing between degrees of discouragement in life experiences, and he acknowledges that a more severe degree of discouragement can stunt emotional growth and functioning.

When the sense of inadequacy overwhelms the individual, far from stimulating him to useful activity, it makes him depressed and incapable of development.[19]

In Adler's thought it is this severe form of discouragement that produces the debilitating inferiority complex and the appositive superiority complex. A person afflicted with a superiority complex loses or does not develop social feeling, community feeling, or social interest; that is, she develops antisocial characteristics. Her striving is for attaining the personal superiority that seeks to dominate others, not for making a greater contribution to the community. This individual is one who seeks the classic power over-and-against others instead of power with others. Adler calls this "neurotic perversion," and postulates that it stems from feelings of extreme humiliation, insecurity, and diminished self-esteem.[20] King is similarly concerned about the effects of severe forms of inferiority and superiority complexes on intragroup dynamics of the blacks. In a statement reminiscent of Adler's view of "power-over-and-against" behavior, King laments the abysmal level of trust among black leaders.

Negroes are capable of becoming competitive, carping and, in an expression of self-hate, suspicious and intolerant of each other. A glaring weakness in Negro life is lack of sufficient mutual confidence and trust. Negro leaders suffer from this interplay of solidarity and divisiveness being either exalted excessively or grossly abused.[21]

He understands the conflict and infighting among black leaders as a symptom of their individual attempts to overcome their inferiority complexes and appear or feel like somebodies. He decries, for example, the behavior of "some Negro clergymen who are more concerned about the size of the wheelbase of their automobiles than about the quality of their service to the Negro community."[22] King diagnoses this behavior as symptomatic of a complex that exalts the self above others in order to feel superior in spite of a deep-seated inferiority complex.

Powerlessness and Self-esteem in King's Thought

Along with the ethnic and feminist thinkers already examined, King is keenly aware of powerlessness as a major contributor to the low self-esteem of the African American oppressed and, by analogy, to the low self-esteem of all oppressed. He essentially considers the history of African Americans as a consistent, persistent, systematic experience of debility; the result is what Korean *Minjung* theology calls han.[23]

Minjung theology describes *han* as the collective experience of chronic, excruciating, oppressive, unrelenting, unbearable, tormenting, unjust, unfair, insufferable, unjustifiable pain over a long period of time. This torturous pain breeds collective and individual resentment, bitterness, explosive rage, and mass psychosis. "It is a dominant feeling of defeat, resignation, and nothingness . . . a feeling of helpless suffering and oppression . . . in the collective social biography of the oppressed Minjung of Korea."[24]

King presages Minjung theology's insight on *han* when he says this of the African American experience of powerlessness:

> The central quality in the Negro's life is pain—pain so old and so deep that it shows in almost every moment of his existence. It emerges in the cheerlessness of his sorrow songs, in the melancholy of his blues and in the pathos of his sermons. The Negro while laughing sheds invisible tears that no hand can wipe away. In a highly competitive world, the Negro knows that a cloud of persistent denial stands between him and the sun, between him and life and power, between him and whatever he needs.[25]

The powerlessness described here breeds a sense of futility, resignation, anomie, nobodiness, and worthlessness of the self. It was in his quest to heal this emotional and psychological devastation that King launched his civil rights movement across America. On the need for African American empowerment, King is clear:

No one can deny that the Negro is in dire need of this kind of legitimate power. Indeed, one of the great problems that the Negro confronts is his lack of power. From the old plantations of the South to the newer ghettos of the North, the Negro has been confined to a life of voicelessness and powerlessness.[26]

By "this kind of legitimate power," King means economic and political power. He believes that power has been abused by its brokers to oppress African Americans and to destroy their self-esteem. He envisions a two-pronged attack on the power-lessness problem. First, he proposes an educational program to repair the ravaged self-esteem of African Americans; and second, a sociopolitical program to organize and mobilize blacks to acquire economic and political power.

King conjectures that unless African Americans gain power to change the oppressive social arrangements, their self-esteem will remain captive to economic and political currents, and that any improvement will be illusory. In this estimation, he cannot be more correct. The "Black Is Beautiful" movement of the 1960s, which evaporated as the economic and political climate worsened in the 1970s and 1980s, bears witness to King's insight. King sees the participation of African Americans in the economic and political mainstream as empowering to them and reparative of their tortured self-esteem.

King's Views on the Nature and Purposes of Power

On first blush, King's views on the nature and purposes of power seem straightforward and uncomplicated; on closer examination, a more complex picture emerges. King defines power as "the ability to achieve purpose. It is the strength required to bring about social, political or economic changes."[27] The perspective on power offered by this statement is consistent with King's belief that the wielding of sociopolitical power by the oppressed is both a safeguard against their oppression and ameliorative of their tormented selves. In this sense, King conceives of the acquisition of power by the oppressed as an instrument of change, and as a bulwark against abusive behavior by the oppressors. Psychologically, power would safeguard against psychic trauma.

King's conception of power grows more involved when he introduces love and justice to the matrix. He states, "Power at its best is love implementing the demands of justice. Justice at its best is love correcting everything that stands against love."[28] This introduction of the metaphors of love and justice infuses the discussion of power with ethical and moral precepts. Indeed, King decries what he sees as the wielding of conscienceless power by European Americans and powerless morality by African Americans.[29] He sees both as immoral and destructive of racial justice. He advocates instead a sharing of creative and positive political and economic power that promotes justice.

In blending the metaphors of power, love, and justice, King is thinking ontologically about the nature of each. In particular, he draws on the thought of Paul Tillich.[30] Tillich's view is that each one of these three metaphors has ontological grounding. By this, Tillich means that each one is "rooted in being itself."[31] Tillich sees ontology as the attempt to analyze and describe what it means to be, and to uncover "the structures . . . common to everything that is, to everything that participates in being."[32]

> One cannot deny that being is one and that the qualities and elements of being constitute a texture of connected and conflicting forces. This texture is one, in so far as it is and gives the power of being to each of its qualities and elements. . . . Ontology is the attempt to describe this texture, to reveal its hidden nature. . . . One cannot escape ontology if one wants to know. For knowing means recognizing something as being. And being is an infinitely involved texture, to be described by the never-ending task of ontology. . . . Love, power, and justice are ever repeated subjects of ontology.[33]

King understands Tillich to insist that "the core of philosophy is the ontological question, and [that] this ontological question is logically prior to every other. Thought must start with being; it cannot go behind it."[34] Three of the philosophical issues that engage King are power, love, and justice, which Tillich believes are inherently ontological. The topic of interest here is power as King understands it.

For King, as for Tillich, power is ontological in the sense that it "plays an important role in the description of ultimate reality";[35] that is, it confers beingness on that which is. In order to be, something must have power. "Being is the power of being!"[36] In order for one to be human at all, one must be endowed with power; this is the ontological principle that King propounds when he decries the powerlessness of African Americans. They cannot be truly human without "the will to power."[37]

As interpreted by King's mentor Tillich, this Nietzschean concept is not the simple, sociopolitical "ability to achieve purpose;"[38] it is, rather, the "self-affirmation of a being in spite of non-being."[39]

> Here we are at the roots of the concept of power. Power is the possibility of self-affirmation in spite of internal and external negation. It is the possibility of overcoming non-being. Human power is the possibility of man to overcome non-being infinitely.[40]

As a major advocate of self-esteem, King has this ontological view of power in mind when he says,

> Black Power is a psychological call to manhood. For years the Negro has been taught that he is a nobody, that his color is a sign of his biological depravity, that his *being* has been stamped with an indelible imprint of his inferiority, that his whole history has been soiled with the filth of worthlessness. All too few people realize how slavery and

racial segregation have scarred the soul and wounded the spirit of the black man. The whole dirty business of slavery was based on the premise that the Negro was a thing to be used, not a person to be respected.[41]

This statement summarizes King's view that powerlessness decisively contributes to African American feelings of worthlessness or shriveled self-esteem. The African American individual is afflicted with *personal* powerlessness, *racial* (group) powerlessness, *sociopolitical* (economic and political) powerlessness, *spiritual* powerlessness, and, finally, *ontological* powerlessness. According to King, the African American individual feels like a nobody. The color of her skin symbolizes racial depravity and degeneracy. Her biography points to social worthlessness in the community of other humans. He is a thing, not a person. His whole being is null and void. That is, the African American individual lacks the power of the "possibility of self-affirmation in spite of internal and external negation . . . [or] . . . of overcoming non-being."

The healing of these feelings of worthlessness, shriveled self-esteem, and tormented sense of self-worth resulting from this ontological nothingness was King's urgent concern. He spent his own life trying to heal the "scarred . . . soul and wounded spirit of the black man."[42] But that is not all; he expended his life trying to heal the soul of the nation that had produced the social leprosy that corroded the souls of the oppressor and the oppressed alike. The result of this leprosy was that the oppressor lacked moral and ethical capital and enjoyed a false sense of self-worth. The oppressed felt devalued and lacked a any sense of self-worth.

FOUR

PASTORAL CAREGIVING AS SHAPED BY KING'S CONSTRUCTIVE THOUGHT

It is not sufficient that we heal suffering persons; we must also be concerned about healing the suffering communities such persons come from and return to. The goals of pastoral caregiving must include a vision of the optimally functional society whose evocative symbol provides quintessential norms for intervention.

So far we have discussed and evaluated various schools of thought as they bear on the issues of identity and self-esteem among the oppressed. These schools have spanned the gamut of critical social theory, philosophy, theology, and psychology. An effort was made to bring into conversation the insights of various thinkers on identity and self-esteem with those of King. The purpose of this mutual interrogation was to clarify King's perspectives so that the latter can inform heuristic models for pastoral care and counseling. This is the task of this chapter and the next. The presentation is rooted in King's constructive thought as distilled from its encounter with other thinkers so far presented. Proposals are based on this constructive thought.

Three major tasks attend the presentation of the proposals. The first is to explicate the norm around which pastoral caregiving must revolve when it is based on an application of King's constructive thought. The second is to explicate its evocative symbol. The third and final effort is a description of the various goals or tasks of pastoral caregiving that are faithful to King's constructive thought as interpreted in this book.

Three norms relevant to pastoral caregiving based on an application of King's thought are discernible: *the theological, the anthropological, and the psychological.* These are the criteria by which pastoral caregiving based on his thought must be tested.[1]

According to King, God is the overarching, cosmic reality and being. By this, King means that there is no perceptible or conceivable reality beyond God, and that God is creator and governor and sustainer of all things. This is standard Christian theology, not unique to King. Further, God is the consummate personality. Herein lies the seeds of King's personalism. King does not mean by this that God is a person in the human sense, possessing human limitations. He means that God exhibits human qualities of empathy, feeling, presence, attentiveness, agency, will, wrath, and judgment, and can be experienced as such. It is in this sense that God is religiously relevant. Still, God's humanlike qualities are infinite, without limit, and perfect beyond reproach. This gives God not only religious relevance, but also adequacy and supernumerarity.

> I studied philosophy and theology at Boston University under Edgar S. Brightman and L. Harold De Wolfe. . . . It was mainly under these teachers that I studied personalistic philosophy—the theory that the clue to the meaning of ultimate reality is found in personality. Personalism's insistence that only personality—finite and infinite—is ultimately real strengthened me in two convictions: it gave me metaphysical and philosophical grounding for the idea of a personal God, and it gave me a metaphysical basis for the dignity and worth of all human personality.[2]

Further, God's personality inheres in the fact that it gives value and worth to creation. All creation has God-value because it was created by God, who confers significance. Personality is ontological, and God is the quintessential personality, supreme and perfect. The ontological status of personality discloses ultimate cosmic reality; the supremacy and perfection of God's personality reveals the worth, dignity, and value of the human personality derived from God's own.[3]

From this theological norm it follows ineluctably that the human is *imago dei*, endowed with some of God's attributes, and bequeathed the value, worth, and dignity of God's personality. This norm applies equally to all humans regardless of race, color, nationality, or social status. This follows from the fact that human personality is a copy of God's personality and is unthinkable without this divine inheritance.

> The sacredness of human personality is the major theme of King's anthropology. According to him, all persons are created in the image of God and, therefore, have inherent worth and dignity. Philosophically, this view is rooted in his personalistic interpretation of human persons. Personalism claims that personality is the clue to reality. For personalists, personality is not only the key to reality, it also has ontological status, i.e., the process that creates persons is also personal. God is the supreme person and the supreme value in the universe. The sacredness of human personality, therefore, has its ground and being in the person of God.[4]

First and foremost in King's thought is the notion that the human psyche is a metaphysical copy of God's psychic structure. Since God is the exhaustive cosmic structure of the universe, the human psyche also has ontological status. Yet the human personality, while moored in God's own, is culturally embedded and shaped. Its health or illness is largely a result of cultural forces that can be perversely deleterious. Culture and its institutions can twist, contort, split, bruise, corrupt, and "thingify" human personality. Such abuse is a direct affront to God's own essence and personality.

Segregation stands diametrically opposed to the principle of the sacredness of the human personality. It debases personality. . . . The tragedy of segregation is that it treats men as means rather than ends, and thereby reduces them to things rather than persons. . . . But man is not a thing. He must be dealt with, not as an "animated tool," but as a person sacred in himself. To do otherwise is to depersonalize the potential person and desecrate what he is. So long as the negro is treated as a means to an end, so long as he is seen as anything less than a person of sacred worth, the image of God is abused in him and consequently and proportionately lost by those who inflict the abuse.[5]

Based on the norms just explicated, four tasks are evident: *reclamation, conciliation, transformation,* and *transcendence.* Before each task can be considered, a word on individualistically oriented pastoral caregiving tasks may be in order.

Hyperindividualistic pastoral caregiving theory and practice has focused its attention primarily on three tasks: *healing, sustaining,* and *guiding.*[6] It conceives of *healing* as the remedial task of repairing harm done, the removal of a disabling condition and the restoring to health of that which may have been harmed. *Sustaining* is conceived as bringing to a problematic situation or suffering persons the resources that will support them until they remobilize to overcome the problem.

Hyperindividualistic pastoral caregiving views *guiding* as the task of helping distressed individuals choose alternative ways of coping without resolving the problem or distress at hand. Wimberly usefully adds that guiding can also entail helping distressed persons to identify and employ alternative coping skills that may not be obvious or apparent to them.[7] Clebsch and Jaekle have added the task of *reconciling* to the tasks just considered. They also postulate a dynamic view of healing as forward-moving, not regressive or static, in which human finitude and divine grace are simultaneously experienced. *Reconciling* aims at mending relational rifts between persons and between persons and God so that the estrangement can be removed and harmony restored. An application of King's thought subsumes and affirms these time-honored tasks of pastoral care and counseling, but also stretches and deepens them.

Reclamation: Pastoral caregiving shaped and expanded by an application of King's thought aims at reclamation at the same time that it promotes healing. In individualistic pastoral care and counseling, healing performs a remedial and restorative role. It has a reparative function. Its principal utility is the treatment of the symptom.

In this book, the two issues are the fractured sense of self or identity and the diminished self-esteem of the oppressed. Groups oppressed on account of sex, race, and class overwhelmingly exhibit these symptoms.

An application of King's constructive thought suggests an approach to pastoral caregiving that goes beyond healing the symptoms of fractured self-concept and diminished self-esteem. His thought points to enabling the symptom-bearer to *reclaim* the sense of somebodiness that issues from being a copy of God's own image and personality. When shaped by an application of King's thought, pastoral caregiving aids the sufferer to achieve more than remedial, restorative, or reparative relief. It aids and supports a deeper adventure to reclaim God-valued, God-worthed, God-dignified, and God-bequeathed personhood, psyche, and personality that has been shackled, twisted, and crippled by oppression. While healing and symptom management aim at restoring the existential and functional status quo, reclamation aims at recovering the divine legacy stolen by oppression.

As stated, reconciliation is one of the four tasks of individualistic pastoral caregiving. The goal of reconciliation is to mend ruptured interpersonal relationships, as well as the relationship with God. An application of King's thought subsumes this in its advocacy of integration as a way of effecting interpersonal and communal harmony.[8]

Conciliation: Pastoral caregiving applying King's constructive thought goes beyond reconciliation to embrace *conciliation* as one of its tasks. Conciliation differs from reconciliation in that its aim is to overcome the hostility or suspicion of the opponent. It seeks to win over or secure the friendship of the opponent, not simply to repair a broken relationship. King's nonviolent stance was a strategy for winning over those opposed to his views and activities. It was a way of building community by dissolving enmity and forging interpersonal and intergroup fellowship. When King's thought is interpreted and applied to the vocation of pastoral caregiving, it is not sufficient for pastoral counseling to *reconcile* one to others and to God. It must also *conciliate* one to oneself and to others. It must promote befriending the worst in oneself and others.

Transformation: Individualistic pastoral caregiving does not list or discuss *transformation* as one of its tasks; but the art and task of pastoral caregiving shaped by an interpretation and use of King's constructive thought requires it. As conceived here, transformation refers to changing the condition, nature, or character of persons and society so that the old is replaced by the new. It is the bringing about of a new order that may incorporate some aspects of the old but whose predominant quality is novelty. When shaped by an application of King's thought, pastoral caregiving achieves its transformative goal if it transforms the oppressed from being things or feeling "thingified" into being and feeling fully human; from being objects into being subjects of their history; from being nobodies into being somebodies. This requires a revolution in habits of thought and behavior. It also requires a processive, not static, view of God. God cannot always be seen as a changeless or change-hating deity who loves all status quo and hates all change. The doctrine of transformation I espouse here requires that we conceive God as a hater of life-denying and health-destroying status quo and a lover of life-affirming and health-promoting change. God loves life, affirms health, and promotes biophilic and salugenic (health-giving) communities. God will not sit impassively and impassionately in the face of death-dealing status quo. Emotional, psychological, and spiritual death is equally displeasing to God. In the face of these diabolic forces, God becomes not changeless but a change agent for the good and for health.

Of course, in order to accommodate this new human creature, society also must undergo a transformation from violence, hatred, exploitation, and abuse of people to justice, love, peace, and equality. Transformation of persons must be accompanied by the transformation of society and its institutions. This model of pastoral caregiving mandates the transformative healing of both human and societal psyches. The healing of one without the other is meaningless, since the untransformed will continue to be a source of psychic toxicity.

Transcendence: Hyperindividualistic pastoral caregiving does not recognize *transcendence* as one of its tasks. Transcendence is a doctrine of classical theology used analogically to refer to the otherness or out-there-ness of God; the connotation is that of a being that stands over against the world and finite beings. God hovers beyond the created order. This is usually contrasted with the doctrine of divine immanence, which refers to the presence, nearness, or indwelling of God in the created order. An application of King's thought to pastoral caregiving embraces both the transcendence and immanence of God. "He is tough-minded enough to transcend the world; he is tender-hearted enough to live in it. He does not leave us alone in our agonies and struggles. He seeks us in dark places and suffers with us in our tragic prodigality."[9]

For the vocation of pastoral caregiving shaped by an application of King's thought, *transcendence* focuses on the inexhaustibility of divine reality, which infuses the human *spirit.* That is, as *imago dei,* the human capacity for self-transformation and actualization cannot be limited by any humanly imposed standard. No human norm can be the measure of wellness or excellence-in-being because human norms are limited, exhausted, and evacuated by sin. The sinful oppressor cannot be allowed to become the norm for the oppressed. Only the transcendence of God can provide the norm for the self in its quest for healing and meaningful living. God's transcendence inspires and enables the oppressed to surmount humanly imposed limitations in the path to life in the kingdom here on earth and to surpass the self in seeking and achieving excellence. With God as the inexhaustible transcendental reality and motive force, the oppressed humanity can tap into that reservoir in its claim to the fullness of life.

Understood as a task of pastoral caregiving shaped by an application of King's thought, transcendence implies caregiving that empowers the oppressed to aspire beyond the norm of the oppressor's personhood and personality, corrupted and twisted as it is by sin. The oppressed can be empowered to tap into the inexhaustible and self-emptying reality of the divine that alone provides the essential and existential norm. This resolves the dilemma faced by the oppressed of idealizing and idolizing the oppressor as representative of the divine. Doing so is patent idolatry and sinful on the part of the oppressed who revere the oppressor, and on the part of the oppressor who requires and demands such reverence.

The Evocation Symbol of Pastoral Care and Counseling as Shaped by an Application of King's Constructive Thought

A symbol is a complex representational concept. It can be an object, idea, word, or perception that represents, vividly and economically, a reality too complex to grasp. The symbol organizes what otherwise would be a diffuse, obscure and, sometimes, unfathomable reality. For example, the cross captures for the average Christian the complex reality of human sinfulness, the self-emptying love of God, and the sacrificial love of Christ.

A symbol, moreover, points to a reality beyond. It points us to something beyond itself at the same time that it uses itself to proclaim that reality. The symbolism of the cross, for example, points us to the salvific efficacy of Christ, the redemptive power of the Resurrection, and the in-breaking of God's kingdom in God's own time, in which humans are summoned by faith and as disciples to participate as redeemed carpenters after Christ.

A symbol can be a highly charged metaphor. Emotionally, it can enliven or deaden, inspire or repel. While the hooded white robes and burning cross of the Ku Klux Klan can inspire a member of the American Nazi Party to zealous fellowship, these symbols predictably strike terror in the hearts of African Americans and Jews. Intellectually, a symbol can engage interminably. Volumes have been written on the theological meaning and significance of the cross. A symbol can also actuate us into fanatical activity or action. In the defense of the American flag which, for some, symbolizes freedom and democracy, the United States has waged some unwise wars and dropped the atomic bomb on Japan.

In sum, a symbol can engage the deep recesses of our beings. It can arouse our intellectual, emotional, and exertive passions. This is the evocative power of a symbol. It is the symbol's power and ability to set our minds, hearts, and actions onto that which it represents, and to give us a reason and standard for heeding its evocation.[10]

Hyperindividualistic pastoral caregiving has not found it necessary to offer an earthly evocative symbol to guide its vocation. The focus has been on the individual sufferer. The therapeutic assumption is that attention to the guiding, healing, sustaining, and reconciling tasks will alleviate the symptoms and enable the bearer of those symptoms to become functional and productive once again. It has seemed unimportant to address the question of what social forces may have conspired to precipitate the symptoms, and how the same forces prohibit or diminish optimal functioning and productive living. In short, the question of how the pervasive sociocultural forces might provoke and reproduce symptomatology has not been the central concern of the individualistic model of pastoral caregiving as shaped by the perspectives of Hiltner, Clebsch, and Jaekle. The work and writing of Howard Clinebell since the 1970s have been devoted to correcting this shortcoming.[11] In addition to Clinebell, feminist, ethnic, and non-Western psychologists and social critics helpfully address this question.

It is a central proposal of this book that pastoral caregiving shaped by King's thought must attend to the social criticism embodied by King's life inasmuch as his life and thought are a paradigm of social criticism. Such an inquiry leads one to an evocative symbol of pastoral care and counseling inasmuch as King's thought supplies it. That symbol is the "beloved community," King's metaphor for a transcendent social order.

In King's thought, the beloved community is heaven incarnate. It is an inclusive community here on earth. For the concrete American polity of which King spoke, integration was synonymous with inclusivity. The beloved community was, therefore, a society that had achieved optimal integration, not just desegregation. For King, a desegregated society was not synonymous with an integrated one. A desegregated society was one where legal sanction for separateness had been removed. An integrated society was unitive. It had achieved a sense of human togetherness and solidarity and was vigilantly intentional about promoting human togetherness. The beloved community is, therefore, an integrated society. In King's thought, such a society was akin to the biblical dominion of God, as King understood that metaphor.[12]

The purpose of this book is not an exhaustive exposition of all the salient features of the beloved community. It is to urge that King's conception of the beloved community furnishes an evocative symbol for giving care to the oppressed and the marginalized. It furnishes a compelling vision of a society rid of social leprosy, a society that creates and promotes an environment in which individual personalities can best prosper. The root metaphors of peace, justice, and love furnish the essential catalysts for healing and eternal wellness; that is, the beloved community is a transformed society committed to justice, peace, and love. Its citizens are transformed persons, imbued with a passion for peacemaking, justice, and love. The soul of such a society is healed by its love of justice and peace and kept healthy by its passion for love, justice, and peace. The psyches of its citizens are likewise healed and nurtured by the fact that they are peacemakers and justice seekers. The process by which the root metaphors of peace, justice, and love transform and heal the souls of both society and persons derives from King's unique understanding and articulation of these metaphors. They constitute the core of the beloved community as an evocative symbol.

King holds a conception of peace that exceeds the popular understanding. The common notion of peace is the absence of war or strife. It is the absence of riots, social unrest, revolution, civil war, terroristic attacks, international war, or general upheaval. King denounces this strifeless peace as false peace or negative peace. He argues that this kind of peace depends on the acquiescence of the oppressed to the forces of evil. It thrives on repression or suppression. For example, African American acquiescence to segregation and discrimination in this society in order to keep the peace or not rock the boat is not peace in King's thought. It is contained violence. Such peace obscures obscene oppression, exploitation, and dehumanization. It is ungodly and contributes to unspeakable pain, suffering, and sorrow. This kind of peace corrodes and corrupts the social fiber at the same time that it twists and torments the human psyche. It is insufferable, diabolical, and intolerable.

In King's thought, true peace has three main characteristics. It is *creative, processive*, and *pacific*. King sees creative peace as resulting from a dialectical tension between the forces of evil and those of light. This kind of peace exposes social and systemic evils so that these can be attacked and eliminated. This kind of peace is, for King, the product of a dialectic that begins with a thesis, which is opposed by an antithesis, resulting in a synthesis. The thesis is the entrenched oppression. The antithesis is the opposition of the oppressed to oppression. The synthesis is any resultant accord or concord. To the extent that the concord is arrived at freely and fairly, it has no equal in spiritual and moral excellence over acquiescence rooted in repression. The latter is the specialty of the race system or racism. It rejoices in acquiescence, not peace. It demands silence, not voice. It employs terror, repression, and suppression in achieving acquiescence, not conversation, dialog, or debate. What it gets is not peace but deeply resented submission, sufferance, and subservience. As a social reality, this state of affairs produces rage, resignation, resentment, self-renunciation, self-surrender, and self-effacement on the part of the oppressed. It produces fear, suspicion, distrust, and mistrust between the oppressed and the oppressors. In King's view, this clearly is not peace. It would be hard to disagree.

King's view of *processive* peace stems from his embrace of nonviolent resistance as both a philosophy of life and a tactic for social change. He does not believe that one can achieve peace by employing nonpeaceful means. For him the two are contradictory. True peace can be achieved only when the *process* of change is itself peaceful. In this view, peace itself becomes a method of achieving peace. For King, it is immoral and wrong to wage war in order to achieve peace. Whatever he may have believed earlier about "just wars" had vanished by the time of his death.

King's third conception of peace stems from religious convictions and is akin to the biblical peace that "passeth all understanding," the peace of God. King believes that the human psyche needs peace as much as does the human community. The beloved community is, of course, the highest and finest expression of such a community. It is a society at peace with itself and the world, one that is devoid of obscene pockets of poverty; a society that loves justice and righteousness. King discerns a restlessness or anxiety of spirit of his age which, he believes, stems from disquieting social conditions of greed, materialism, war, and injustice.

Pastoral caregiving shaped by an application of King's views on peace attends to overt and covert social strife that produces psychic trauma in the human. The root metaphor of peace or its absence blends with King's view that the human personality, though divinely endowed, is socially embedded; the social institutions and systems shape its health or pathology. A society at war with itself or others cannot nurture healthy human emotions. The identity conflicts and diminished self-esteem of the oppressed reflect, in King's thought, chronic social war being waged against them. These disorders stem from the peaceless existence of the oppressed, and from their inability to take charge of their existence.

One prerequisite, therefore, to alleviating the identity and self-esteem problems of the oppressed is to *wage* social peace. This challenges pastoral caregiving to be as concerned about the health of the social psyche as it is about the human psyche. In particular, it challenges caregivers to work as vigorously for societal peace as for repairing the wounded psyches of the psychologically and emotionally afflicted.

King's life and work reveal a preoccupation with a utilitarian concept of justice, that the morally right and just action is that which promotes the greatest social good. The principal exponent of this concept of justice is John Stuart Mill.[13] Mill's recitation of instances of unjust actions resonate with King. These include depriving people of their legal and moral rights, punishing the innocent instead of the guilty, treating unequally persons in the same or similar circumstances, favoritism, and breaking faith with the people.[14]

King also embraces an Aristotelian concept of distributive justice wherein people are treated according to their legitimate claims. However, for King, persons' legitimate claims include the sanctity of their person and persons attached to them. It also includes an equitable distribution of economic goods. On the question of the latter, King modifies the Aristotelian formulation to include the needy citizen whose legitimate claim includes whatever she needs for a life with a reasonable degree of comfort and personal dignity.

It is this embrace of traditional notions of fair play and substantial justice that impelled King to seek more just laws, to disobey those laws he considered unjust, to seek welfare benefits for the abject poor and the unemployed, and to work to eliminate segregation and discrimination.

King, however, goes two steps further than the classicists in his conceptualization of justice. He embraces justice as *righteousness* and justice as *participatory* or *sociopolitical.*

In advocating the concept of justice as *righteousness,* King is again drawing on the depths of his spiritual life. He is proclaiming the justice of God on earth. In doing so, he is equating justice with human rights based on his belief in the sacredness and inviolability of the human personality created in the image of God. He is simultaneously embracing the prophetic teaching that a person's claim to know God is hollow unless one does justice or righteousness.[15] The Hebrew word *mishpat* is rendered "justice"; *tsedaqah* is rendered "righteousness."[16] "Mishpat consists in doing justice to the poor, neither more nor less."[17] King correctly believes that the justice of God requires a particular sensitivity to the demands and requirements of the oppressed poor.

King expands these notions of justice to incorporate the idea of social justice as participation by the oppressed poor in the decision making that affects their lives. Under this rubric, it is not sufficient for the oppressed poor to benefit from distributive justice. The poor and powerless also must participate in the productive process, and in decisions on how the socioeconomic pie is divided and distributed.

Pastoral caregiving informed by King's views on the nature and efficaciousness of justice insists that society do justice to the oppressed poor, and the oppressed poor must be empowered to seek justice in the service of health and wellness. It must also insist that the oppressed poor participate in the decision-making process of the socioeconomic order. Two rationales attend this requirement. In King's thought, the identity and self-esteem of the oppressed are affected by their feelings of powerlessness and worthlessness. Their marginalization contributes to their feelings of powerlessness and worthlessness. Their participatory activities affirm their humanity and heal their symptoms.

Participation in the decision-making processes of society can give them a sense of belonging that is critical to their feelings of self-worth and somebodiness. It also allows them to participate in the wielding of social power critical to their empowerment. Engaging in productive activities can also enhance their diminished self-esteem. Their self-concept can equally improve from the feeling that they belong to a human community that values them and their contributions, and that treats them as human beings, not things. The oppressed can experience their subjectivity, not only their objectification. Their fractured senses of self can heal by identifying with their God-given personhoods, not with the pseudo humanity of the oppressors that has been refracted and distorted by sin. Their self-worth can mend from being in control of their destinies.

King distinguishes among three senses of love: *eros, philia,* and *agape.* Of the three, he is most influenced by his understanding of *agape.* He defines *agape* as "redeeming good will for all men," which he sees as self-giving and sacrificial Christian love. King does not equate agape with liking those who opposed him personally or his ministry to the oppressed. He believes only that agape allows him to search for whatever is positive in people and to transform a stranger into a neighbor. His model for this stance is the parable of the good Samaritan in Luke 10:33.[18] The salient question posed by this parable is not "What will happen to me if I come to the aid of the afflicted?" but "What will happen to the afflicted if I do not come to his aid?" The parable, therefore, requires today's Christian to confront the most central tenet of her faith. For, not only does it seek to save us from a narcissistic preoccupation with the self, it also reminds us of Jesus' own ministry on earth. Jesus asked himself the same question that the good Samaritan asked of himself and responded by coming to earth that we might be saved.

Especially relevant to the vocation of pastoral caregiving is King's view that "agape is disinterested love"; that it "does not begin by discriminating between worthy and unworthy people, or any qualities people possess."[19] Implicit in this statement is the unconditional positive regard a pastoral counselor must possess in order to work with the oppressed as a class of people.

This status-blind agape creates a positive milieu in which real healing takes place. While this can occur at an interindividual level, King's concern is the group-dynamics or community level. This is the level at which the practice of agape, as King explicates it, creates a social milieu in which humans can extend unconditional positive regard to one another, and allow broken souls and psyches to heal and flourish. Pastoral caregiving shaped by an application of King's thought challenges us to attend to these social dynamics as a way of serving the oppressed, who may not access the privatistic model.

An application of King's thought on agape to the vocation of pastoral caregiving challenges the vocation further. King sees agape as effectuating another salugenic outcome. It is promotive and creative of community. This is both a secular and a spiritual community, in which God's personality is manifest and in which human personalities can flourish as in a loving family.

> *Agape* is love seeking to preserve and create community. It is insistence on community even when one seeks to break it . . . . Agape is a willingness to go to any length to restore community . . . . The cross is the eternal expression of the length to which God will go in order to restore broken community. The resurrection is a symbol of God's triumph over all the forces that seek to block community. The Holy Spirit is the continuing community . . . . I can only close the gap in broken community by meeting hate with love. If I meet hate with hate, I become depersonalized, because creation is so designed that my personality can only be fulfilled in the context of community.[20]

King's insistence on agape as a forger of community and on community as the healer of brokenness implies two additional pastoral caregiving goals. It liberates pastoral caregiving from the private to the public arena, where brokenness is shared and where healing is a matter of communal concern. Public psychiatry becomes the indicated modality. King's insistence also underscores the public nature of the human personality and the necessity to be as concerned about healing the commonwealth as the private person. In this perspective, the community becomes the arena for experiencing the familyhood that decisively molds personality. "Another basic point about agape is that it springs from the *need* of the other person—his need for belonging to the best in the human family."[21]

King's insistence also points to the therapeutic value of receiving and giving love. In agapeistic exchange both the givers and receivers of love enjoy wholeness of personality because God, the ultimate personality, is at the center of the healing process experienced in community, and the Holy Spirit is the quintessential community. The utter centrality of agapeistic community for the healing of human brokenness, or the prevention of such, is accented by King's perspective, articulated here. Pastoral counselors are affirmed as they give agapeistic care. The oppressed are affirmed and healed as they receive agapeistic care. The Holy Spirit as the encompassing community infuses all human interactions with transformative possibilities. The key is that all this takes place in the public arena, where the norm is God as the ultimate personality.

For King, nonviolence was both a philosophy or ethic, which guided his life commitments, and a method for social and human transformation. As a philosophy or ethic, it is informed and motivated by his deep respect for the sacredness of the human personality, and his refusal to violate that sacredness by harming or destroying it. King believes that human personality derives from God's own, and is God's bequest. It is unthinkable that a human being can intentionally harm or destroy that which is divinely endowed. He also believes that violence corrupts and corrodes the souls of the perpetrator and the victim. No one is spared the degrading impact of violence. The victim lives in morbid fear of destruction and suffers a tormented psyche and stunted personality development. The perpetrator suffers warped values and a deformed personality, since she hates and destroys that which is very much a part of herself.

As a philosophy, King's views on nonviolence derive from Mahatma Gandhi's *patyagraha* (Truth-Force), which King adapts to mean Love-Force. Thus, King is able to reinforce his views on nonviolent resistance with the views on agape just considered. Agape extends the redemptive, self-sacrificial love of Christ to the otherwise nonlovable or unlikeable. Christ nullified that classification because he died for the sinful man that he might be redeemed and enjoy the love of God. Nonviolence puts into practice what the heart feels and the soul believes. It offers its practitioner's own body and life as a sacrifice so that the other person's divinely derived worth and dignity can be spared and preserved. The motifs of both agape and nonviolence are tied to a reverence for the human personality and a refusal to desecrate it.

As a method of transforming self and society, King sees nonviolent resistance as a way to minimize bloodshed, irrational violence, and hate. As a practical matter, the forces of darkness overwhelmingly outpower the forces of light. There is no match between the two in destructive capacity. Additionally, King seeks to communicate that the object of his campaigns was not to defeat the opponent but to win her over. Tactically, this saves the opponent's face and ego, and tames her irrational reaction. King also sought to prick the opponent's conscience so that the opponent could change her ways before inflicting bloodshed.

King distinguishes between nonviolent resistance and passivity, or do-nothingness. The former is a powerful and effective armory of resistance. It does indeed resist overwhelming official power arrayed against it. It is a method of the tenacious and the brave, not those lacking in courage and fortitude.

Pastoral caregiving shaped by an application of King's views on nonviolence discerns three parameters for itself. The first one concerns the way in which nonviolence affirms the personalities of both the resister and the resisted. Neither one is degraded. The nonviolent resister does not degrade himself by taking sacred life. On the contrary, he affirms himself by practicing agape. Healing occurs in the moment of numinous intersection between preserving the sacred entrustment and self-emptying. Did not God in Christ empty Godself that brokenness might heal and sinful natures be redeemed? Did not Jesus enflesh that which God had decreed and ordained? The nonviolent resister incarnates God's will that life be affirmed and nurtured. The opponent benefits from God's ordinance that, despite himself, forgiveness and grace are extended and available. King's root metaphor of nonviolence requires that the pastoral care movement promote nonviolence as a philosophy of social organization, and as means of healing human brokenness.

FIVE

THE PRACTICAL APPLICATION OF KING'S THOUGHT

The concept of health is broader than personal and human. It includes societal and ecological health. Toxic social systems and ecologies cannot produce healthy psyches. The concern of pastoral caregiving must include the health of societal and ecological psyches which shape and sculptor human psyches.

This chapter proposes a model for pastoral caregiving shaped by an interpretation and application of King's constructive thought. The indicated model is *community* pastoral caregiving, with its two aspects: *ecological* and *public policy* pastoral caregiving.[1] "Ecological" is used here in a broader sense than its twin concept of "environmental." Usually the two are used interchangeably and confusingly. "Environment" usually carries a spatial-static connotation as the sum total of external conditions and circumstances affecting the existence and functioning of life. "Ecology" is used here to connote the dynamics of the environment, the relationship between organisms and their environment. Appropriated is the interactive, relational sense of ecology suggested by James W. Fowler[2] when he talks about the "ecology of care" and the "ecology of vocation" and uses each conceptually to suggest an interactive and transformative relationality. Ecological pastoral caregiving embraces this dynamic and includes in its vision caregiving that takes place at different levels of human ecology, and whose vocation is the formation and transformation of persons, communities, systems, and structures. Implicit in this conception of ecology is the belief that such transformation and reformation will be salugenic, not pathogenic.[3]

King's thought, presented in the preceding chapters, moves caregiving to oppressed communities away from the hyperindividualistic model to a serious analysis of sociocultural environments that oppress and distress. Community pastoral caregiving shaped by King's constructive thought must engage these sociocultural environments, and intervene to change the toxic systems and structures that disturb individuals and groups instead of focusing on providing relief to disturbed individuals only. The focus of this model is on the caregiver's skill at systems analysis, and the designing of intervention modalities based on that analysis, rather than on a preoccupation to change the behavior or personalities of the afflicted.

The question of the exact causes of emotional and psychological distress is a complex one, beyond the scope of this book. In chapter 1, I presented the various presuppositions of pastoral theology, medical neurology, and modern psychiatry concerning the etiology of mental distress. Community pastoral caregiving begins with a serious engagement with persons in their contexts as the fundamental axiom for the assessment and understanding of human distress. The relevance of biochemistry and genetics is seriously acknowledged but not accorded etiological ultimacy. On the contrary, it is the relevance of the environment and the interaction between it and the sufferer as an active and acting agent that is presumed to be the defining factor in mental disturbance. This person-in-context approach asks both what is wrong with the sufferer and how he can be helped, as well as what might be wrong with the sufferer's setting and how altering the setting might change his symptomatic behavior. Asking the latter question avoids the bias of the hyperindividualistic model, which removes persons from their contexts as it seeks to understand the cause of their distress. It further compels an analysis of the sociocultural structures and systems that conduce or intensify emotional and psychological distress.

This approach to pastoral caregiving is consistent with five collateral insights. The first of these is King's view of the utter social embeddedness of human personhood and personality. King believes that humans are so socioculturally embedded that they cannot usefully be studied or understood apart from that intimate sociality. King's perspective on this issue is akin to the African worldview elaborated by John S. Mbiti in his monograph *African Religions and Philosophy*.

Mbiti explicates an African theological anthropology that is intensely corporate and communitarian. The African man or woman is an image of the creator God and an incarnation of deep corporateness in which one's sense of self and emotional health are intimately connected to a community of the departed (past), the living (present), and the yet unborn (future).

> In traditional life, the individual does not and cannot exist alone except corporately. He owes his existence to other people, including those of past generations and his contemporaries. He is simply part of the whole. The community must therefore make, create or produce the individual; for the individual depends on the corporate group. . . . Just as God made the first man, as God's man, so now man himself makes the individual who becomes the corporate or social man. It is a deeply religious transaction. . . . Whatever happens to the individual happens to the group, and whatever happens to the whole group happens to the individual. The individual can only say: "I am because we are; and since we are, therefore I am."[4]

This sense of communal and corporate embeddedness mirrors King's and affirms the efficacy of community pastoral caregiving.

The second supporting insight is that of Alfred Adler discussed earlier. Adlerian psychotherapy is decisively contextual, ecological, and holistic. It presupposes a context of social embeddedness as the best environment in which to understand persons and their distress. Adler discerned the fundamental human need to be finding a place to belong (community), to complete oneself (achieve integrity of self), and to feel significant (enjoy a healthy self-esteem). In Adler's thought, that place or community is the culture of embeddedness or an ecology of care.[5] Adler's insight also affirms the heuristic efficacy of community pastoral caregiving. It takes seriously the sense of solidarity or fellowship in the human community that a person must have to function healthfully. Adler terms this sense "social feeling" or "community interest." King names it a feeling of "somebodiness." Its lack inevitably precipitates neurosis, understood as a complex of psychiatric disorders in the psychoanalytic tradition that shaped Adler's thought.

The third insight that supports the efficacy of community pastoral caregiving is that of Salvador Minuchin. His family systems theory posits an individual as a subsystem of a social system that is in process of continual interaction or change. At no point is an individual unconnected or unrelated to other social systems or subsystems with which he interacts. The other systems or subsystems might include parental, spousal, child, sibling, or extrafamilial relationships. According to this systemic understanding of human personality, emotional distress can never be a private preserve of the identified patient. It can only be a symptom of a systemwide problem or of a relevant subsystem, organization, community, or family.[6]

In Minuchin's theory, effective psychotherapeutic intervention must aim at altering the structure of the relevant social system or subsystem that is emotionally or psychologically disturbing the sufferer. It is believed that change in the structure of the distressing system or subsystem inevitably alters the immediate context within which interaction occurs, resulting in objective relational transformations. Objective changes ineluctably yield subjective changes in the behavior of the sufferer, leading to symptomatic healing and health. Since objective changes are systemic, they have systemwide impact as well. The resulting interactive changes, also systemwide, heal the individual sufferer, the system or subsystems which produce suffering, and the community that comprises them.[7]

In instances where systemic executive functions are impaired or otherwise dysfunctional, Minuchin's approach empowers the caregiver to enter the system, take over, and model executive functions. This can become necessary in instances where oppressive forces have so ravaged the identified individual patient or systemic patient as to immobilize her.

A blend of Minuchin's insight and community pastoral caregiving shaped by King's thought seems natural. King's own life and work are a case study in social reordering and systemic restructuring in order to undo oppressive arrangements. His goal was to undo and rearrange sociopolitical structures, create pluralistic power-wielding subsystems and, in the process, heal individual and societal suffering. King's thought and work are premised on the conviction that dispersed centers of power subjectively and objectively transform and heal a shackled humanity and community. True to Minuchin's insights, King advocated public assistance programs in order to strengthen executive functions in the households or communities of the oppressed poor.

The fourth insight is that of the World Health Organization's (WHO) perspective on health. An agency of the United Nations, WHO describes health as a "state of complete physical, mental and social well being and not merely the absence of disease or infirmity."[8] It regards "the enjoyment of the highest attainable standard of health as a fundamental right of every human being without regard to race, religion, political belief, economic or social condition." It further connects the enjoyment of the highest standard of health to the attainment of global and international peace and security. WHO urges its member states and individuals to cooperate fully to realize peace and security through health. Our primary interest is in the simultaneous remediation and prevention of emotional and psychological distress among the oppressed. WHO's constitution addresses that concern as well.[9] Article 2, Section (m), of the WHO constitution specifically commits the organization "to foster activities in the field of mental health, especially those affecting the harmony of human relations."[10]

It is evident that the spirit and mission of this respectable international body is very much in accord with a pastoral caregiving perspective inspired by King's life and thought. King's thought too embraces pastoral caregiving that has a keen concern for social peace and justice. In King's thought, peace is a deeper reality than the mere absence of war or social strife. It is the peace that passes all human understanding; it is spiritual peace, the peace of God. WHO also regards health as more than the mere absence of disease or infirmity; it makes a connection between that state of health and global peace. It views the health of individuals and of societies as a vital promoter of peace and security. The two are inseparable and indivisible.

On the specific issue of how WHO's function in promoting mental health might contribute to a peaceable and secure world, David Mitrany has said:

> Psychologists and psychiatrists . . . cannot hope to achieve results in the field of mental health in a world which breeds and lives on prejudice, which produces continuous and widespread states of anxiety, and which periodically subjects individuals and society to the shock of violent conflict.[11]

The vision of social analysis and change evident in pastoral caregiving illumined by an application of King's thought is also evident in Sections (g) and (h) of WHO's constitution, which talk about the eradication of disease and its prevention, respectively.[12] WHO is empowered by its constitution to respond to crisis health situations as well as initiate action to change distress-causing environments so that health can be established, maintained, or promoted. This is to be done in the service of both individual and social wellness. An application of King's thought to the vocation of pastoral caregiving aims at achieving human and social wellness through the agency of agape, peace, and justice previously considered. WHO's vision of a peaceable and secure world is akin to King's conception of the beloved community, a society healed of individual and social leprosy.

Finally, the multisystemic insights of Nancy Boyd-Franklin[13] are a refinement and idiosyncratic application of both Minuchin and King to the psychotherapeutic intervention of suffering African American families. In all five theories considered so far, the elements of public advocacy, education, prevention, and systemic transformation are prevalent aspects of the healing and health of suffering persons and society.

Ecological Dimension of Community Pastoral Caregiving

Community pastoral caregiving shaped by a conversation between King's thought and the other five schools of thought must employ an ecological understanding of maladjustment, and seek causes of maladjusted functioning in the interactive interdependence between the self and the ecology, both human and nonhuman. It must seek to understand how emotional disturbance can be a complex sociocultural, sociopsychological, and sociopolitical phenomenon springing from oppressive social arrangements. Significant stressors include racial, class, and sex oppression, and the absence of effective cultural, economic, and political support systems to aid effective functioning and eradicate systemic toxicity.

Epidemiologic studies that show a prevalence of certain types of mental disorders among women, "nonwhites," and the underclass lend support to this approach, for there appears to be a causal, albeit elusive, link between oppressive factors and certain mental disorders such as, for example, schizophrenia.

In a classic study on the distribution of anxiety and schizophrenia by economic class in the city of New Haven, Connecticut, it was found that, in the representative population sample, the upper class and upper middle class had a psychiatric population of only 7.7 percent, compared with 88.6 percent for the lower middle class, working class, and lower class.[14] A psychiatric population of 3.7 percent was of unknown class. If only the working-class and lower-class samples are considered, their representative psychiatric populations total 75.4 percent, compared with 7.7 percent for the upper class and the upper middle class. Of the upper-class psychiatric population of 1.0 percent, 52.6 percent represent those with neurotic disorders, while 47.4 percent represent those with psychotic disorders. The upper-middle-class psychiatric population shows a prevalence rate of 67.2 percent for neuroses and 32.8 percent for psychoses.[15]

In contrast, the working-class psychiatric population shows a prevalence rate of only 23.1 percent for neurotic disorders, and a significantly high rate of 76.9 percent for psychotic disorders. The lower-class psychiatric population presents a neurotic disorders rate of only 8.4 percent, compared with a very high rate of 91.6 percent for psychotic disorders.[16] It is evident from the study that the neurotic disorders are concentrated in the higher strata of the social order, while the psychotic disorders are concentrated in the lower strata.

When the researchers focused only on schizophrenic patients across the general United States population (with appropriate statistical adjustments for variations in sample sizes), the concentration was startling. The working class and the lower class were represented by a rate of 86.8 percent schizophrenics, compared with a rate of only 13.2 percent for the upper class, upper middle class, and lower middle class combined.[17] A similar study in Chicago confirmed that serious psychiatric disorders, such as schizophrenia, alcohol-related disorders, and others, were heavily concentrated in lower-class neighborhoods.[18] With regard to the psychological disorder of anxiety, the study showed a higher prevalence of these disorders among the upper class (53 percent) than among the underclass (8 percent).

A comparison of the prevalence of mental disorders between the sexes also yields interesting data. Of the population-wide 38 percent schizophrenics admitted to state and county hospitals in the United States in 1980, 42 percent were female and 35 percent male. Mood disorders accounted for 20 percent female and 10 percent male. Admissions related to organic disorders were equal for both female and male at approximately 4 percent.[19]

When data on admissions to private psychiatric hospital inpatient services, as opposed to public institutions, is examined, a different picture emerges. Admissions for mood disorders predominate among females (51 percent), compared with males (34 percent). Admissions for schizophrenia are about equal, at 20 percent for females and 23 percent for males. Admissions for alcohol- and drug-related disorders are higher among males than among females, at 18 percent and 7 percent, respectively. Admissions for organic disorders for both males and females are about even, at 4 percent and 3 percent, respectively.[20]

The racial breakdown of admissions for major psychological disorders reveals an intriguing pattern as focus is directed on the most productive 25 to 44 age group. Of the population-wide 44 percent admissions for schizophrenia, 61 percent were nonwhite; only 37 percent were white. Alcohol- and drug-related admissions were 21 percent nonwhite against 30 percent white. Admissions for mood disorders rated at 7 percent nonwhite and 16 percent white. Rates for organic disorders showed a statistically insignificant difference of 3 percent nonwhite, versus 2 percent white.[21] Of the five groups—upper class, male, underclass, female, and nonwhite—the latter three constitute the focus of this book. I have identified these as the oppressed of the land.

It is noteworthy that the prevalence of schizophrenia in each of these groups is quite high compared to their counterparts. In the New Haven study, it is 88.6 percent for the underclass compared with 7.7 percent for the upper class. Between female and male schizophrenics, the national divide is 42/35 percent. The distribution between nonwhite and white schizophrenics ages 25–44 is 61/37 percent nationally.

The question of the meaning of these epidemiologic studies is a complex one and beyond the scope of this book. While data show a higher prevalence of schizophrenics among the groups that have been identified in this book as the oppressed, this may not prove that oppression causes schizophrenia. Genetic and biochemical factors have been hypothesized in the etiology of schizophrenia.[22] Still, these hypotheses remain speculative, not conclusive findings. Other nonorganic hypotheses have been advanced to explain the origin of schizophrenia.

For example, the sociogenic hypothesis proposes a causal link between schizophrenia and social class.[23] The social-drift theory seeks to link the prevalence of schizophrenics in the lower class to their propensity to drift into this class after being afflicted, not before.[24] These hypotheses are called social causation and social selection, respectively.[25] The school of family theory has contributed the schizophrenogenic mother and the double-bind hypotheses.[26] Whatever the reason for the prevalence of this disorder among the oppressed, it does not appear to be merely coincidental. A useful hypothesis is that oppression itself may be a significant factor in the disordered lives of the sufferers. Just how significant a factor it is, remains to be determined by additional research.

> Schizophrenia is more prevalent among individuals with low socioeconomic status, suggesting that the deprivation and distress associated with this status are risk factors. More epidemiologic research is needed to demonstrate whether low socioeconomic class is a cause of schizophrenia or a consequence. The downward-drift hypothesis suggests that the massive psychological and social impairments associated with schizophrenia result in downward social mobility for most schizophrenic patients. Although this hypothesis is both intuitively compelling and supported by some research, the hypothesis that some aspects of low socioeconomic class contribute to schizophrenia remains viable.[27]

Even though the precise nature of this contribution remains elusive, it does not seem far-fetched to appropriate the view that oppression is a major contributor. This view is bolstered by the epidemiologic data presented above, which tends to show that schizophrenia shows higher levels of prevalence among the other oppressed groups, women and nonwhite. It is not easy to establish genetic or biochemical interconnections among these groups. Witness, for example, the prevalence of mood disorders. The prevalence of this disorder among primarily the upper class and women argues against a genetic, biochemical hypothesis in favor of a sociocultural theory. In a way not entirely clear, the two groups seem to share the experience of anxiety.

Alcohol- and drug-related disorders seem to pattern social habits as well. Males are afflicted in greater numbers than females (34 percent to 12 percent). It would be most difficult to establish a genetic, biochemical nexus between white males and nonwhite males and white females and nonwhite females. Lifestyles, which are similar within each gender group, appear to be a more plausible explanation than genetics. Lifestyle is a sociocultural product, not a biochemical or genetic one. In the area of organic disorders, where social behavior or experience are insignificant factors, prevalence rates are almost identical across the racial, sex, and socioeconomic lines.

Pastoral caregiving shaped by an application of King's thought embraces an ecological perspective on the etiology of certain psychological disorders and on their remediation. This perspective views oppression as the primary contributor to emotional and mental distress due to its capacity to render its victims powerless, at personal and group levels, to mobilize resources with which to prevent, cope with, or remediate distress in their lives.

The relational and interactive dynamic between the disturbed individual and the environment must characterize the assessment, diagnosis, and remediation of maladjustment and its prevention. A commitment to sociocultural transformation must attend the vocation of ecological pastoral care and counseling, in which the issue of powerlessness and empowerment is an urgent concern.

The Factor of Power and Powerlessness in Ecological Pastoral Caregiving

The factor of power and powerlessness preoccupied King's dissection of the anatomy of oppression in the United States. It also informed his insight into the social leprosy that had wrecked African American psychological well-being and continued to thwart it. An ecological perspective on pastoral caregiving must seriously engage the full dimensions of the power dynamic while seeking to give care to the oppressed.

> The topic of powerlessness is of particular relevance for community psychology since it is the relative *absence* of power, or feelings of power, amongst individuals or groups with high rates of psychological distress that is likely to be more apparent to those who work with a community psychology approach than will be the relatively advantaged position of those who wield power.[28]

A sense of *control* over self or events is critical in any assessment of how powerlessness affects the emotional health of the oppressed. The causal link appears to be very strong.

> Let's consider McDougall's *self-assertion*, Maslow's *dominance-feeling*, White's *competence*, de Charm's *personal causation*, Rotter's internal versus external *locus of control*,

Seligman's *learned helplessness,* and Bandura's *self-efficacy.* . . . Each one of these influential concepts has served, in its own way, to identify feelings of personal power as a central component of the human psyche. Furthermore, most have linked feelings of power with psychological health, and feelings of lack of power with mental ill-health or psychological distress.[29]

Among the oppressed, feelings of anomie, alienation, and nothingness stem from their experience and feelings of powerlessness. Feelings of powerlessness, loss of control, incompetency, anomie, or nothingness can contribute to psychological distress inasmuch as they impair the person's coping skills and sense of mastery over life events. This insight helps us better understand why schizophrenic disorders are more prevalent among females, nonwhites, and the underclass than among other groups. It is these groups that invariably feel the debilitating effects of powerlessness and loss of control over their lives. Schizophrenia is the result of maladjustment stemming from impoverished coping skills. It is the natural consequence of extreme privation.

A comparative study of the rates of suicide between the oppressed groups and other groups, presents a confusing picture in terms of any link between the prevalence of emotional and psychological distress among the oppressed and possible self-destruction. That none seems apparent is one of the most puzzling mental health phenomena studied.

In the United States, in the year 1989, the death rate by suicide was 18.6 males and 4.5 females per 100,000 population.[30] It appears that despite the incidences of high prevalence of certain types of serious emotional and psychological distress among females, the rate of those who choose to take their own lives is lower than that of men. This picture crystallizes more clearly when we look at the 15–24 age group, where the relative rates per 100,000 are 22.2 for males and 4.2 for females.[31] The rate per 100,000 for males ages 35–44 is 22.8, compared with 6.6 for females of the same age group. The disparity increases almost exponentially with further advances in age.[32] Possible explanations for this disparity are that females may have stronger ego strengths than males (contrary to the cultural myth of females as the weaker sex), or that the male sense of self is so linked to the control and mastery of social systems and institutions that despair readily sets in once this control and mastery are lost with old age.

The data on suicide rates across the racial line is also striking in its disclosure that European Americans in general take their own lives at higher rates than African Americans. For instance, in the year 1989, per 100,000 population of each group, the rate for European Americans of both sexes who committed suicide was 12.0, compared with a rate of 7.1 for African Americans.[33] Further, 19.6 was the rate for European American males who committed suicide, compared with a 12.5 rate for African American males. And the rate was 4.8 for European American females, compared with a rate of 2.4 for African American females.[34] There is a near-persistent ratio of 2 to 1 in these rates.

These rates per 100,000 population become increasingly striking as advances in age are accounted for. In the same year 1989, a rate of 24.2 for European American males, ages 45 to 54, took their own lives, compared with a rate of only 10.9 for African American males. The relative rates for females were 8.0 for European American and 3.0 for African Americans. In the 65-and-over range, European American males took their own lives at a rate of 43.5, compared with just 15.7 for African American males. The rate for European American females was 6.3; for African American females, it was only 1.8.[35]

Many different definitions of suicide have been offered. Suicidologists have also classified suicide variously. However, Emile Durkheim's definition and classification of suicide continue to command respect among experts.[36] Durkheim's three-part classifications of suicide as "egoistic," "anomic," and "altruistic"[37] have been expanded to include

> rational (to escape pain), reactive (following loss), vengeful (to punish someone else), manipulative (to thwart other plans), psychotic (to fulfill a delusion), and accidental (reconsidered too late).[38]

Egoistic suicide is that which results "when an individual is not strongly integrated into his society"; *altruistic suicide* results when "there is excessive integration of the individual with society and he sacrifices himself, such as the soldier in battle"; *anomic suicide* is that "in which the individual's adjustment to or integration with society is disrupted or unbalanced, as might occur, for example, in times of economic depression."[39]

Shneidman lists the following common characteristics of committed suicide:

> where the purpose is to seek a solution to an intractable problem; where the goal is to cease one's own state of consciousness; where the stimulus is intolerable psychological, not physical, pain—the pain of feeling pain; where the stressor is frustrated psychological needs; where the felt emotion is hopelessness-helplessness; where the internal attitude is ambivalence; where the cognitive state is constriction of affect and intellect; where the action is aimed at escape or egression from a region of distress; where the interpersonal act is communication of intention; and where consistency is with life-long coping patterns.[40]

This conceptuality might shed light on the apparent inconsistency between the epidemiologic prevalence of certain psychiatric disorders among the oppressed groups, which can be viewed as predisposing factors for suicide, and the lower rates of suicide among them. It appears that while predisposition to psychiatric disorders may serve as a contributive factor to suicidal ideation and completion, availability and utilization of coping mechanisms also play a significant role. A sense of solidarity among the oppressed may also mitigate some of the helplessness and hopelessness endemic to their circumstances. The social unacceptability of suicide as a constructive means of solving one's problems may be another inhibiting factor. More cohesive and effective social support systems among blacks may further account for their low rates of suicide, while, for example, a general prevalence of ineffective social support systems has been hypothesized to account for high suicide rates among Native Americans.[41]

Suicide rates in different countries show significant variations in incidence relative to each place, yet what remains consistent is the comparative predominance among male and female, upper class and lower class, white and nonwhite, where applicable, and between the young and very old. In the majority of these categories, findings in the United States hold true of most countries of the world.[42]

Closely related to this ecological dynamic of community pastoral caregiving is an appreciation for the desirability of diversity in all human communities. That no social order is unicultural seems axiomatic. The melting-pot view of the social order is discarded, not only because it is a fictitious construct, but also because assimilation is a symptom of sociocultural intolerance and imperialism. It annihilates desirable diversity in the human and physical ecology and promotes and maintains maladjustment among the powerless oppressed. In the place of assimilation, the model of ecological pastoral caregiving embraces a *salad bowl* perspective of the human ecology, which celebrates diversity held in balance and blend. The vocation of pastoral caregiving moored in a celebration of diversity must attend to a constant alteration of systemic structures to maintain or promote *salad bowl* diversity.

Ecological pastoral caregiving shaped by an application of King's thought must also embrace the view of the human as having inherent potential for achievement of competency. This is the ability to modify and change the self, when given the opportunity, and to acquire ability to adapt to a salugenic ecology or transform a pathogenic one. No human must be viewed as innately incapable of growth or change. The focus must steer away from a view of the human character as innately defective and toward a view that stresses empowerment for change.

King's life, thought, and work are a stirring appeal to the oppressed to aspire for such ability, and to the oppressive ecologies to aid in the transformative process. A competency model of ecological pastoral caregiving simultaneously remediates existing symptomatology and prevents its recurrence. It empowers the oppressed to master their own destinies, at the same time that it heals the sufferer. It enlists the powerful in this transformative adventure as an expression of their faith in the resurrected Christ and an all-inclusive church, the body of Christ. It heals and enriches society by affording sufferers an opportunity to make salugenic contributions to the common life. The individualistic model's approach of merely relieving individual symptomatology is an inadequate servant of healing or prevention of personal and group distress.

Allied to the ecological dimension of community pastoral caregiving is its emphasis on its public policy twin. This dimension includes the task of advocacy. Its aim is to design and advocate public policies that promote the welfare of all citizens, especially the powerless oppressed. Political participation, change in the laws, and economic justice are at the core of its intervention repertoire. Useful skills in this arena remain systems analysis and design, and the empowerment of the powerless oppressed. The participation of the powerful as an expression of faith and praxis of the gospel ministry must be the guiding motive, consistent with King's dream of an inclusive commonweal. A belief in and commitment to the healing of the souls of society and persons must remain its guiding vision.

This vision is very compatible with the theological perspective that both society and persons are creatures of the one living God who remains interested in the welfare of both. The same God governs and redeems both humans and the created order in such a way that their disparagement damages the somas and psyches of both. Further, such disparagement repudiates the love and will of the living God for life and health. It is clear that an application of King's constructive thought to pastoral caregiving impels the view that community pastoral caregiving is heuristic. The perspectives of Mbiti, Adler, Minuchin, the World Health Organization, and Boyd-Franklin help to clarify two aspects, the ecological and the public policy dimensions.

These perspectives, and King's, direct attention away from the private domain of emotional and mental distress to the contributions of oppressive social systems. These systems decisively ravage both personal and societal psyches. Remediation and prevention strategies must intervene systemically and enlist other ecologies of care to aid in the task of advocacy and change in both suffering individuals and suffering communities, where God's providence suffers as well. The Christian church, as the body and servant of the suffered and resurrected Christ, remains faithful to its mission only when its caregiving remains vigilantly attentive to how social systems and structures, created by humans, oppress persons and communities and intervene to stop and prevent it. Jesus the Christ expended his own life determined to stop such oppression. King expended his own life trying to do the same. The church can do no less.

AFTERWORD

Justice, peace and love metaphors are triplets. You cannot have one
without the other two. Each metaphor must be understood in radi-
cally new ways. Justice must be forged, not only administered. Peace
must be waged, not only kept. Love must be tough, not only tender.
Righteousness must imbue all three.

In this chapter an assessment is made of the chief contributions King's practical theology makes to pastoral caregiving, especially among the oppressed of any context,
and particularly where the Christian faith is practiced.

Chief among these is the fact that even though King's training was in systematic
theology, his life and work reveal a preoccupation with the care and cure of the souls
of both persons and communities. The latter included the American and the global
communities. Toward this task, he employed an array of theological and psychological insights and made a notable contribution to the field of pastoral caregiving.
This aspect of King has never been recognized.

King engaged in systems analysis and in political activism. He sought to change
dehumanizing systems and institutions, to replace oppressive legal codes, to enfran-
chise the disenfranchised, to give a sense of hope to the hopeless, and to make the
nobodies feel like somebodies. He did this in the service of a divinely inspired
evocative symbol, the beloved community. This is an earthly community of the children of God where God's justice, righteousness, and love abound. It is a redeemed
and healed community whose citizens likewise are redeemed and healed because
they are freed from dehumanizing and subhumanizing social forces.

The second intuition unearthed by King's practical theology is that psychological
and emotional disturbance can be understood largely as an interactive dynamic
between the person and oppressive environments rather than as evidence only of
mental illness or disease. This insight leads the diagnostician and caregiver away
from locating causative factors exclusively in the intrapsychic or genetic structure of
the sufferer to an analysis of sociocultural, sociopolitical, and sociopsychological
forces that distress minds and emotions as well as bodies.

Closely related is the proposal that instead of focusing exclusively on individual
sufferers as identified patients, or on specific "diagnostic group aggregates, such as
schizophrenics,"[1] pastoral caregiving should direct attention to ecological aggregates
such as class, sex, race, powerlessness, ethnicity, residential patterns, and support
systems.[2] The focus must be on overall evidence of prevalent symptomatology
rather than on specific individual sufferers. As an example, the question must be
both who the individual schizophrenics are and where and why schizophrenia pre-
dominates.[3]

A third intuition flows from the first two, namely that a fractured or fragmented sense of self, truncated self-esteem, and a sense of anomie and hopelessness are endemic symptomatologies of members of oppressed communities, whether that oppression be based on sex, race, or class. Oppression is an underlying stressor of somas, psyches, and emotions. This book proposes that oppression and deprivation are major contributors to emotional and psychological maladjustment.

A key feature of this intuition is the argument that, as the pastoral caregiving movement seeks to give care to women, racial minorities, and the underclass, it will discover that there are commonalities in the way these groups experience the emotional and psychological phenomena of self-identity and self-esteem. A tortured or fractured self-identity and diminished or shriveled self-esteem are characteristic experiences of the self of the oppressed. A critical search for the cause of this common symptomatology points to oppression as the principal, though not exclusive, contributor to the felt distress. In turn, the oppressive phenomenon discloses common threads in the manner and method by which it is entrenched and perpetuated in the systems and structures of society. This argues in favor of a socially based model of pastoral caregiving with four guiding visions: (1) a clearly envisaged evocative symbol; (2) transformation, transcendence, and conciliation as additional central tasks of pastoral caregiving; (3) systemic and structural change, with the goal of empowerment, as the objective of pastoral caregiving; and (4) individual and social healing as the goal of pastoral caregiving.

The fourth chief contribution to pastoral caregiving that is made by King's practical theology is its intuition that community and public policy pastoral caregiving characterize intervention strategies in working with members of the oppressed communities. This approach has several merits. It is faithful to King's practical theology, life, and work. It validates the overall symptomatological assessment of the problem as dynamically sociopolitical and systemic. It enlists and invests the sufferers in the cause of their own healing. It empowers the afflicted to become subjects of their own biographies instead of being victims thereof. It emphasizes education and prevention rather than relief.[4] It challenges those treatment strategies that aim at effecting relief to individual sufferers, without eliminating the sociocultural roots of distress, to emphasize eradication rather than relief.

The fifth chief contribution is that the public policy metaphor of community pastoral caregiving seeks to change systems in the name of God's continuing work of creation, redemption, and judgment. It affirms the public nature of the vocation of the priest, pastor, and church. It affirms and honors the sacred nature of the human personality by publicly lifting up to God's throne of grace the least of any community, the oppressed of the land.

Finally, the ecological metaphor of community pastoral caregiving affirms the theological understanding of human growth and development as best achieved in an interactive process between self, others, and ecology,[5] where ecology is understood as an interactive dynamic between the human and the environment. Interrelationality, a centerpiece of the vocation of pastoral caregiving, is preserved and promoted by an ecological understanding of distress and its possible remediation.

Examples of Contexts in Which This Community Pastoral Care
Model Has Been Applied

———

Intuitions developed from King's practical theology concerning how best to give care to the oppressed groups and communities were tested by King himself when he pastored Dexter Avenue Baptist Church in Montgomery, Alabama. Among the many innovative programs King instituted at Dexter, three were specifically aimed at socially empowering the parish and the community he served so that both might heal from centuries of subhumanization and be restored to health. The blend between social and spiritual empowerment was intimate.

Shortly after his installation as Dexter's pastor, King caused to be formed the Social and Political Action Committee (SPAC). The primary purpose of this committee was to empower eligible African Americans, long terrorized into not voting, to register and exercise their rights as citizens to vote. During King's time in the 1950s, and before passage of the Voting Rights Act of 1965, citizens of Alabama were required to pay poll taxes in order to qualify to register to vote. Even after payment of poll taxes, qualifying to vote in Alabama was a complex and treacherous process, riddled with many pitfalls along the way. Any slight misstep rendered an African American instantly ineligible to vote. Even persons with bachelor's or advanced degrees did not feel confident that they could successfully navigate the murky waters of the registration process.

Dexter's SPAC studied the registration process and conducted workshops for church members and the general community to guide them through the registration process. The explicit agenda behind SPAC's function was to remove the terror from the exercise of one's civic rights. Its other agenda was, however, to empower the nobodies into somebodies, and to actually increase African American political power, which at that time in Alabama was negligible. The strategy worked.

Dexter Baptist Church became identified with unexcelled civic and political leadership. Its self-esteem as a congregation soared as never before. It produced individuals whose self-esteem also soared. These persons ran for local political offices in Montgomery or left to lead major organizations elsewhere in the nation. Shortly thereafter, Dexter became the seat of the Montgomery Improvement Association (MIA), which organized and for 381 days led the boycott of the segregated Montgomery bus system. With the intervention of the Supreme Court of the United States, the bus system was desegregated. As a result of the success of this event, both King and Dexter were instantly catapulted into the national and international limelight. To date, Dexter and its membership continue to enjoy the pride and esteem of this historic past. Indisputably, SPAC made a significant contribution to repairing the self-esteem of many African Americans in Montgomery and the rest of Alabama. The civil rights movement it incubated undeniably elevated the self-esteem of its participants to uncharted heights as it made them feel that their humanity was beginning to be acknowledged.

The second activity King engaged in while at Dexter was to mobilize the congregation and the African American community to establish their own credit union. It was King's conviction that African American individual and group self-esteem would increase in direct proportion to their ownership of successful business ventures, especially financial institutions. Of course, there were African Americans in Montgomery who owned and operated small businesses such a hair salons, restaurants, barber shops, taxi cabs, neighborhood grocery stores, and other mom-and-pop establishments. There were doctors and lawyers and other professionals as well. However, there were no African American major business enterprises or financial institutions. King felt that this was a major lack for several reasons.

In the first place, it made it nearly impossible for African Americans to procure capital to finance major business ventures or homes. It prevented African Americans from developing any real sense of how financial institutions operate. In a general sense it prevented them from developing the self-confidence one acquires from successfully operating a business enterprise, especially a financial institution. King felt that the self-esteem that would accrue from the ownership and management of a financial institution was worth the hassle it would take to organize one. For almost three years, King and a committee composed by him worked tirelessly to organize an African American credit union in Montgomery. It appears that he met with relentless opposition from persons both in Alabama and Washington, D.C., who felt threatened by the idea. By the time of his resignation from Dexter the credit union idea, though still throbbing, was essentially dead.

Simultaneous with the credit union King also organized another committee to explore the idea of an African American hospital in Montgomery. Even though an enormous amount of time and energy was spent developing plans for the hospital, the project floundered on King's departure for Atlanta to head the SCLC from there. Consistent with his practical theology, King believed that ownership and operation of a hospital was necessary in order for African Americans to repair their distorted self-identities and repair their fractured self-esteem. Individually and corporately, they needed to participate fully in the life-blood of this nation of which the economic system was key. They also needed to break the psychology of dependency on European Americans for everything, including health.

A similar conviction currently drives the KIDSHOPPE at Community Presbyterian Fellowship in Birmingham, Alabama. The ostensible purpose of the KIDSHOPPE is to train children ages six through thirteen to learn how to start and operate a business of their own through the use of biblical and theological concepts. These children are primarily, if not exclusively, from an inner-city neighborhood with chronic socioeconomic problems. Most of the children come from low-income, single parent homes. Practically none of them knows a person who owns or operates a business of any kind. The vast majority of these children's parents receive welfare benefits.

The venture provides hands-on instruction in how to establish and manage a business, and provides them with conceptual tools for entrepreneurship. Discipline, responsibility, and accountability are instilled. Self-sufficiency and capitalistic values of competitiveness and market economics are taught, including an awareness of the global economy. The children operate a convenience store, where they market drinks, candy, bread, milk, and food products to area residents.

For inner-city children and their parents entirely unexposed to how businesses are formed or operated, this experience is empowering. The children's self-concept as potential members of an achieving society is planted and clarified. They can identify as members of an enterprising community, not merely as consumers. They can identify as owners and operators of what society values and derive self-value in the process. They can invest themselves in the useful activity of building an economic enterprise and take pride in its success. They can see the fruits of their labor and learn lifetime management skills. Their self-esteem can repair and grow as they become aware of their usefulness to the community and society as contributing members, as opposed to being primarily its dependents. They can feel like somebodies as opposed to feeling like nobodies. The children's response to KIDSHOPPE has been ecstatic. They exude pride, hope, enthusiasm, and constructive behaviors where listlessness and negativism previously reigned.

Of kindred spirit to the KIDSHOPPE is the BIG WHAM WHAM project in Titusville, Alabama. This project is located in another inner-city neighborhood previously left vacant and deteriorating. A committee of neighborhood residents, organized to raise money, purchased a dilapidated building that was an unmitigated eyesore. They renovated and transformed it into a neighborhood grocery store that is community owned and operated. BIG WHAM WHAM provides area residents with basic grocery needs at economical cost. It also provides employment to area residents who were previously unemployed and unemployable.

The planning process, which required input from a committee of area residents, was a classic study in community empowerment and consciousness raising. Persons who previously had never served on a board or community organization of any kind found themselves visioning their economic future together. The collaborative efforts of previously dispirited persons, whose only witness was the deterioration of their neighborhood and the dilapidation of its structures, was salvific. It has transformed their perception of who they are and their capacity to effect change in their lives. It has transformed their assessment of their own power as a community of persons with a destiny contrary to the message of hopelessness they had been hearing. A real sense of self-sufficiency emerged from the interdependence the project spawned, accompanied by pride in their accomplishment. It is this feeling of self-ownership and self-authorship that King's practical theology envisioned as ameliorative of fractured self-identities and self-esteem of the oppressed.

In this book, I have endeavored to propose a sociotheological, oppression-sensitive model of pastoral caregiving. It is a compelling model that springs from my conviction that, in the face of manifest social oppression, the vocation of pastoral care and counseling can ill afford to remain largely privatistic or hyperindividualistic in its theory or practice. Integrity of vocation requires that oppressive social forces be confronted and dismantled lest they overwhelm the God of life, health, and justice and devastate the psyches of humanity and society.

NOTES

Introduction

1. For a detailed transcript of King's life, see "Chronology," in Martin Luther King Jr., *The Words of Martin Luther King, Jr.: Selected by Coretta Scott King* (1958; reprint, New York: Newmarket Press, 1983), 99–110. See also James Melvin Washington, "Martin Luther King, Jr., Martyred Prophet for a Global Beloved Community of Justice, Faith, and Hope," in *A Testament of Hope: The Essential Writings of Martin Luther King, Jr.*, ed. James M. Washington (San Francisco: Harper and Row, 1986), xviii–xix. This resume was abstracted primarily from these two sources.

2. King, "Chronology," 99.

3. Ibid., 100.

4. Ibid.

5. Washington, "Martin Luther King, Jr.," xix; and King, "Chronology," 100.

6. King, "Chronology," 101.

7. Ibid., 101–02.

8. Ibid., 107.

9. See Martin Luther King Jr., *Stride Toward Freedom: The Montgomery Story* (New York: Harper and Row, 1958); *Strength to Love* (New York: Harper and Row, 1963); *Why We Can't Wait* (New York: Harper and Row, 1963); *The Trumpet of Conscience* (New York: Harper and Row, 1968); and *Where Do We Go From Here: Chaos or Community?* (New York: Harper and Row, 1967).

10. E. Brooks Holifield, *A History of Pastoral Care in America: From Salvation to Self-Realization* (Nashville: Abingdon, 1983), 191.

1. The Anatomy and Patterns of Oppression

1. See Gerda Lerner, *The Creation of Patriarchy* (New York: Oxford University Press, 1986); Mary Daly, *Beyond God the Father* (1973; reprint, Boston: Beacon Press, 1985); and Paul Enns, *The Moody Handbook of Theology* (Chicago: Moody Press, 1989).

2. Enns, 38–43.

3. Tertullian, as quoted in Daly, *Beyond God the Father*, 44.

4. Daly, *Beyond God the Father*, 44. Sprenger and Kraemer were German professors of theology to whom Pope Innocent VIII wrote in 1484 commissioning them as inquisitors to eradicate witches and witchcraft. In 1486, these two theologians codified in the *Malleus Maleficarum* ("Hammer of Witches") the ecclesiastical rules for detecting acts of witchcraft. See William A. Clebsch and Charles R. Jaekle, *Pastoral Care in Historical Perspective: An Essay with Exhibits* (Englewood Cliffs, N.J.: Prentice Hall, 1964), 191.

5. See Rosemary Radford Ruether, *Sexism and God-Talk: Toward a Feminist Theology* (Boston: Beacon Press, 1983), 82.

6. John Calvin, *Commentaries on the First Book of Moses Called Genesis*, vol. 1, trans. John King (Grand Rapids: Eerdmans, 1948), 129, as quoted in Lerner, 183.

7. Lerner, *Creation of Patriarchy,* 18.

8. Sigmund Freud, "Some Physical Consequences of the Anatomical Distinction Between the Sexes" (1925), in *The Standard Edition of the Complete Psychological Works of Sigmund Freud,* vol. 19, trans. James Strachey (London: Hogarth Press, 1961), 248–58.

9. Freud, "Some Physical Consequences," 257.

10. *Civil Rights Act of 1964, Statutes at Large,* 78, sec. 88-352, 241–68 (1964).

11. U.S. Bureau of the Census, *Statistical Abstract of the United States: 1991,* 111th ed. (Washington, D.C.: GPO, 1991), 386.

12. Information presented at a seminar conducted by the National Conference of Christians and Jews, sponsored by the School of Theology at Claremont, 27–28 October 1988.

13. *Information Please Almanac: Atlas and Yearbook, 1992,* 45th ed. (Boston: Houghton Mifflin, 1992), 34.

14. United Nations, *The World's Women 1970–1990: Trends and Statistics,* Social Statistics and Indicators, Series K, no. 8 (New York: UN, 1991), 32.

15. Joan Chittister, *Job's Daughters: Women and Power* (New York: Paulist Press, 1990), 52.

16. "Vatican Declarations," Origins, N.C. Documentary Service, VI (3 February, 1977), 522, quoted in Jacquelyn Grant, *White Women's Christ and Black Women's Jesus: Feminist Christology and Womanist Response* (Atlanta: Scholars Press, 1989), 26.

17. Daly, *Beyond God the Father,* 19.

18. Emmanuel Doronzo, *Sacraments of Orders,* quoted in Catherine Beaton, "Does the Church Discriminate Against Women on the Basis of Their Sex?" Critic 24, no. 6 (June–July 1966): 22. "The reason . . . for denying women the right to teach is a reason that is absolute and universal, based as it is on the natural condition of inferiority and subjection that is the portion of women. . . . This moral feebleness is manifest at once in the lightness of judgment, in credulity . . . and finally in the fragility of spirit by which she is less able to rein in the passions, particularly concupiscence."

19. Chittister, *Job's Daughters,* 21–22.

20. United Nations, *The World's Women,* 45.

21. Chittister, *Job's Daughters,* 74.

22. Edith Sandes, "The Hamite Hypothesis: Its Origin and Functions in Time Perspective," *Journal of African History* 10 (1969): 521–32. See also Charles B. Copher, "The Black Man in the Biblical World," *Journal of the Interdenominational Theological Center* 1, no. 2 (Spring 1974): 7–16.

23. Copher, "Black Man in the Biblical World," 7.

24. Benjamin Quarles, *The Negro in the Making of America* (New York: Macmillan, 1964), 71. "Catechisms for the religious instruction of slaves commonly bore such passages as: 'Q: Who gave you a master and a mistress? A: God gave them to me. Q: Who says that you must obey them? A: God says that I must.'"

25. See Thomas F. Gossett, *Race: The History of an Idea in America* (Dallas: Southern Methodist University Press, 1963), 17–83. See also John S. Haller Jr. *Outcasts from*

Evolution: Scientific Attitudes of Racial Inferiority, 1859–1900 (Urbana: University of Illinois Press, 1971).

26. Robert V. Guthrie, "The Psychology of Black Americans: An Historical Perspective," in *Black Psychology,* 2d ed., ed. Reginald L. Jones (New York: Harper and Row, 1981), 17.

27. Basil Davidson, *The African Slave Trade* (Boston: Little, Brown and Co., 1980), 28–29.

28. John Henrik Clarke, "The Caribbean Antecedents of Marcus Garvey," in *Marcus Garvey and the Vision of Africa,* ed. John Henrik Clarke (New York: Vintage Press, 1974), 17.

29. Walter Rodney, *How Europe Underdeveloped Africa* (Washington, D.C.: Howard University Press, 1974), 97.

30. Davidson, *African Slave Trade,* 68.

31. U.S. Dept. of Labor, Bureau of Labor Statistics, *Employment and Earnings,* vol. 38, no. 12, December 1991 (Washington, D.C.: GPO, 1991), 25.

32. National Conference of Christian and Jews, seminar materials.

33. Ibid.

34. U.S. Bureau of the Census, Current Population Reports, *Poverty in the United States: 1990,* Series P-60, no. 175 (Washington, D.C.: GPO, 1991), 16–17. In the U.S., the poverty line for 1990 was an income of $13,359 per year for an urban family of four.

35. National Conference of Christians and Jews, seminar materials.

36. Derrick Bell, *Civil Rights: Leading Cases* (Boston: Little, Brown and Co., 1980), 1–64.

37. Charles V. Hamilton, "On Parity and Political Empowerment," in *The State of Black America, 1989* (New York: National Urban League, 1989), 114.

38. See E. Franklin Frazier, *The Negro Church in America,* 23–26, and C. Eric Lincoln, *The Black Church Since Frazier* (New York: Schocken Books, 1974).

39. Frazier, *Negro Church in America,* 33–51.

40. See Carter G. Woodson, *The Mis-Education of the Negro* (1933; reprint, Washington, D.C.: Associated Publishers, 1972).

41. Edwina C. Johnson, "An Alternative to Miseducation for the Afro-American People," in *What Black Educators Are Saying,* ed. Nathan Wright Jr. (New York: Hawthorn Books, 1970), 198–205.

42. Ibid., 199.

43. Ibid., 200–01.

44. Ibid., 201–02.

45. *Report of the National Advisory Commission on Civil Disorders* (New York: Bantam Books, 1968), 203–04.

46. Cynthia Tucker, "Behind Bars," *Atlanta Journal/Atlanta Constitution,* 17 January 1993, G7.

47. Ibid.

48. Ibid.

49. U.S. Bureau of the Census, *Poverty in the United States: 1990,* 4.

50. Ibid., 15.

51. Man Keung Ho, *Family Therapy with Ethnic Minorities* (Beverly Hills, Calif.: Sage Publications, 1987), 18.

52. Ibid., 16–17.

53. Ibid., 14.

54. Salvatore R. Maddi, *Personality Theories: A Comparative Analysis*, 4th ed. (Homewood, Ill.: Dorsey Press, 1980), 10–14.

55. Ibid., 14.

56. Daniel K. Lapsley and Kenneth Rice, "The 'New Look' at the Imaginary Audience and Personal Fable: Toward a General Model of Adolescent Ego Development," in *Self, Ego and Identity: Integrative Approaches*, eds. Daniel K. Lapsley and F. Clark Power (New York: Springer-Verlag, 1988), 116.

57. Ibid.

58. See Susan Sturdivant, *Therapy with Women: A Feminist Philosophy of Treatment*, Focus on Women 2 (New York: Springer Publications, 1980), 85–94.

59. See Marcia Westkutt, *The Feminist Legacy of Karen Horney* (New Haven: Yale University Press, 1986), 114.

60. See ibid.

61. Freud, "Some Physical Consequences," 257.

62. Miriam Greenspan, *A New Approach to Women and Therapy* (New York: McGraw-Hill, 1983), 94–95.

63. Harriet Goldhor Lerner, "Is Family Systems Theory Really Systemic? A Feminist Communication," in *A Guide to Feminist Family Therapy*, ed. Lois Braverman (New York: Harrington Park Press, 1988), 47–63.

64. Ann Wilson Schaef, *Women's Reality: An Emerging Female System in a White Male Society* (San Francisco: Harper and Row, 1985), 23–50.

65. Ibid., 36–67. See also Jean Baker Miller, *Toward a New Psychology of Women* (Boston: Beacon Press, 1986), 19–20: "In fact, women are encouraged to believe that if they do go through the mental and emotional struggle of self-development, the end result will be disastrous—they will forfeit the possibility of having any close relationships. This penalty, this threat of isolation, is intolerable for anyone to contemplate. For women, reality has made the threat; it is by no means imaginary."

66. "Another important result is that subordinates (i.e., the oppressed) often know more about the dominants than they know about themselves. If a large part of your fate depends on accommodating to and pleasing the dominants, you concentrate on them. Indeed there is little purpose in knowing yourself. Why should you when your knowledge of the dominants determines your life?" Miller, *Toward a New Psychology for Women*, 6–7.

67. Ibid., 83.

68. Carol Gilligan, *In a Different Voice: Psychological Theory and Women's Development* (Cambridge: Harvard University Press, 1982), 173–74.

69. Ibid., 173.

70. Theo Witvliet, *A Place in the Sun: An Introduction to Liberation Theology in the Third World* (Maryknoll, N.Y.: Orbis Books, 1985), 47.

71. Ibid.

72. Frantz Fanon, *Black Skin, White Masks,* trans. Charles L. Markmann (New York: Grove Press, 1967), 109–10.

73. Ibid., 154.

74. Ibid., 63.

75. Ibid., 167, 170.

76. *Three Negro Classics: Up from Slavery, Booker T. Washington; The Souls of Black Folk, William E. B. DuBois; The Autobiography of an Ex-Colored Man, James Weldon Johnson* (New York: Avon Books, 1965), 214–15.

77. "The individual can only say: 'I am, because we are; and since we are, therefore I am.' This is a cardinal point in the understanding of the African view of man." John S. Mbiti, *African Religions and Philosophy* (Garden City, N.Y.: Doubleday, 1970), 141.

78. See, for example, Celia Jaes Falicov, "Mexican Families," Nydia Garcia-Preto, "Puerto Rican Families," and Guillermo Benal, "Cuban Families," in Monica McGoldrick, John K. Pearce, and Joseph Giordano, eds., *Ethnicity and Family Therapy* (New York: Guilford Press, 1982), 134–163, 164–186, 187–207.

79. Paul Tillich, *The Courage to Be* (New Haven: Yale University Press, 1980), 166.

80. Ibid., 164.

81. Ibid., 164–65. "One could say that the courage to be is the courage to accept oneself as accepted in spite of being unacceptable. One does not need to remind the theologians of the fact that this is the genuine meaning of the Pauline-Lutheran doctrine of 'justification by faith'. . . . Accepting acceptance though being unacceptable is the basis for the courage of confidence."

82. Nyameko Pityana, "What Is Black Consciousness," in *The Challenge of Black Theology in South Africa,* ed. Basil Moore (Atlanta: John Knox Press, 1974), 61.

83. Paulo Freire, *Pedagogy of the Oppressed,* trans. Myra Bergman Ramos (New York: Continuum Publishing, 1983), 28.

84. Ibid., 28.

85. Ibid., 30.

86. Ibid., 30.

87. Ibid., 31.

88. Ibid., 31.

89. Ibid., 33.

90. Alfred Adler, "Early Recollections and Dreams," in *The Individual Psychology of Alfred Adler: A Systematic Presentation in Selections from His Writings,* eds. Heinz L. Ansbacher and Rowena R. Ansbacher (New York: Basic Books, 1956), 358.

91. Linda Tschirhart Sanford and Mary Ellen Donovan, *Women and Self-Esteem* (New York: Penguin Books, 1984), 7.

92. Ibid.

93. Sanford and Donovan attribute this definition to William Appleton.

94. Lee P. Brown, "Crime in the Black Community," in *The State of Black America, 1988* (New York: National Urban League, 1988), 99.

95. William H. Grier and Price M. Cobbs, *Black Rage* (New York: Basic Books, 1980).

96. Sanford and Donovan, *Women and Self-Esteem,* 415.

97. Schaef, *Women's Reality,* 23.

98. Freire, *Pedagogy of the Oppressed,* 30.

99. Grier and Cobbs, *Black Rage,* 178.
100. Sturdivant, *Therapy with Woman,* 112–13.
101. Schaef, *Women's Reality,* 133–34 (emphasis added).

2. King's Perspective on Identity Formation and Its Problems

1. King, *Where Do We Go from Here,* 43.
2. Adler was a member of Freud's inner circle in the latter's evolving psychoanalytic movement in late-nineteenth-century Vienna. He broke ranks with Freud in 1911 to launch his own individual psychology movement which, unlike the Freudian emphasis on the biological determinism of human personality, emphasized its social embeddedness.
3. Alfred Adler, *Understanding Human Nature* (New York: Greenberg Publishers, 1946), 72. "Striving for superiority" was one such pathology, and a major one in Adler's system.
4. Pityana, "What Is Black Consciousness?" 60–61.
5. In his sermon "Antidotes for Fear," King alludes to Freud's view of neurotic phobias as intrapsychically grounded. See King, *Strength to Love,* 117.
6. Ibid.
7. Martin Luther King Jr., "The Ethical Demands for Integration," in *A Testament of Hope,* 122.
8. King, *Where Do We Go from Here,* 99.
9. Ibid., 97.
10. Ibid.
11. See especially James W. Fowler, *Stages of Faith: The Psychology of Human Development and the Quest for Meaning* (San Francisco: Harper and Row, 1981); "Stages of Faith and Adult Life Cycles," in *Faith Development in the Adult Life Cycle,* ed. Kenneth Stokes (New York: W. H. Sadlier, 1983), 179–207; "Faith and the Structuring of Meaning," in *Faith Development and Fowler,* eds. Craig Dykstra and Sharon Parks (Birmingham: Religious Education Press, 1986), 15–42; *Becoming Adult, Becoming Christian: Adult Development and Christian Faith* (San Francisco: Harper and Row, 1984); and *Faith Development and Pastoral Care* (Philadelphia: Fortress Press, 1987). See also Jerome Beryman, ed., *Life Maps: Conversations on the Journey of Faith, Jim Fowler and Sam Keen* (Waco, Tex.: Word, 1978); and James Fowler and Robin W. Lovin, eds., *Trajectories in Faith* (Nashville: Abingdon Press, 1980).
12. Fowler, *Stages of Faith,* 98–116.
13. Ibid., 5.
14. Ibid., 9–15.
15. Fowler, "Stages of Faith and Adult Life Cycles," 181.
16. Fowler, *Stages of Faith,* 92–93. Later reformulations and refinements which, however, preserve the essential and original meaning, can be found in *Becoming Adult,* 74–75; *Faith Development in the Adult Life Cycle,* 179–80; and "Faith and the Structuring of Meaning," 25–26.
17. Fowler, "Faith and the Structuring of Meaning," 16.
18. Ibid., 21.

19. Ibid., 23.
20. Fowler, "Stages of Faith and Adult Life Cycles," 180.
21. Fowler, "Faith and the Structuring of Meaning," 15–42.
22. King, *Where Do We Go from Here*, 97.
23. Fowler, "Stages of Faith and Adult Life Cycles," 180.
24. Fowler, *Stages of Faith*, 98.
25. See Erik H. Erikson, *Childhood and Society*, 2d ed. (New York: W. W. Norton, 1963); *Identity, Youth and Crisis* (New York: W. W. Norton, 1968); *Identity and the Life Cycle* (New York: W. W. Norton, 1980); and *Dimensions of a New Identity* (New York: W. W. Norton, 1974).
26. The correlation between Freud's psychosexual and Erikson's psychosocial stages can be readily gleaned from the following chart:

Erikson's Stages	Freud's Stages
Trust vs. Mistrust	Oral
Autonomy vs. Shame, Doubt	Anal
Initiative vs. Guilt	Phallic
Industry vs. Inferiority	Latency
Identity vs. Role Confusion	Genital
Intimacy vs. Isolation	Same
Generativity vs. Stagnation	Same
Ego Integrity vs. Despair	Same

See Erikson, *Childhood and Society*, 273.
27. Ibid., 268–69.
28. Ibid., 250–51.
29. In *Childhood and Society*, 241–46, Erikson attempts to take into account the unique and peculiar tribal experiences of the Native Americans and African Americans in explication of his identity theory.
30. Robert Kegan, *The Evolving Self: Problem and Process in Human Development* (Cambridge: Harvard University Press, 1982), 3–4.
31. Ibid., 138–39.
32. Ibid., 82–83.
33. Ibid., 100.
34. Ibid., 294.
35. Ibid., 28.
36. Ibid., 81–82.
37. Ibid., 121–32. It is instructive that the "holding environment" performs a greater differentiative and less integrative role as the individual develops from incorporative, impulsive, imperial, interpersonal, and institutional to interindividual evolutionary truces. In relation to the truces, the cultures of embeddedness are: mothering, parenting, role recognizing, mutuality, identity or self-authorship, and intimacy, respectively. Significantly, the cultures of embeddedness shift from being primarily private to being primarily public as the person traverses the constructive-developmental path. That is, the confirmatory, contradictory, and continuitory influences of the public domain become critical for a healthy sense of self as the person attains greater age. In this theory, psychopathology results from the absence or dysfunctioning of

the holding environments to perform their appropriate roles during each evolutionary truce or motion.

38. "Individual" names a current state of evolution, a stage, a maintained balance or defended differentiation; "person" refers to the fundamental motion of evolution itself, and is as much about that side of the self embedded in the life-surround as that which is individuated from it. The person is an "individual" *and* an "embeddual." Ibid., 116.

3. King's Thought on Powerlessness and Self-Esteem among the Oppressed

1. James H. Cone, *A Black Theology of Liberation* (Philadelphia: J. B. Lippincott, 1970), 27–28.
2. King, *Where Do We Go from Here*, 122.
3. Ibid., 123.
4. Martin Luther King Jr., "Where Do We Go from Here," in *A Testament of Hope*, 245.
5. Martin Luther King Jr., "The Ethical Demands for Integration," in *A Testament of Hope*, 121. In short, it is the problem of being beautiful but not *feeling* beautiful.
6. King, *Where Do We Go From Here*, 43.
7. King, "Ethical Demands for Integration," 121.
8. Ibid., 122.
9. Adler, "Striving for Superiority," in *The Individual Psychology of Alfred Adler: A Systematic Presentation in Selections from His Writings*, ed. Heinz L. Ansbacher and Rowena R. Ansbacher (New York: Basic Books, 1956), 117.
10. Ibid., 101–26.
11. Ibid., 126–62.
12. This rendering of the German word *gemeinschaftsgefuhl*, as connoting more than "social feeling" is offered by Walter Beran Wolfe in Adler, *Understanding Human Nature*, 31–32, n. 1.
13. Adler, "Early Recollections and Dreams," 358.
14. Alfred Adler, *Superiority and Social Interest: A Collection of Later Writings*, eds. Heinz L. Ansbacher and Rowena Ansbacher (New York: Viking Press, 1964), 91.
15. Martin Luther King Jr. "Nonviolence and Racial Justice," in *A Testament of Hope*, 5–6.
16. King, *Where Do We Go from Here*, 109–10.
17. King, *Strength to Love*, 116.
18. Ibid., 117.
19. Alfred Adler, "The Neurotic Disposition," in *The Individual Psychology of Alfred Adler*, 258.
20. Adler, "Striving for Superiority," 108–09.
21. King, *A Testament of Hope*, 307.
22. King, *Where Do We Go from Here*, 36.
23. See Suh Kwang-Sun David, "A Biographical Sketch of an Asian Theological Consultation," in *Minjung Theology: People as the Subjects of History*, ed. Commission on Theological Concerns, Christian Conference of Asia (Maryknoll, N.Y.: Orbis Books, 1983), 15–37.

24. Ibid., 24–26.

25. King, *Where Do We Go from Here*, 102–03.

26. Ibid., 36.

27. Ibid., 37.

28. Ibid.

29. Ibid.

30. King wrote his dissertation on the thought of Paul Tillich and Henry Nelson Wieman by comparing their conceptions of God. See Martin Luther King Jr., *A Comparison of the Conceptions of God in the Thinking of Paul Tillich and Henry Nelson Wieman*, Ph.D. dissertation, Boston University, 1955 (Ann Arbor: UMI, 1977).

31. Paul Tillich, *Love, Power and Justice: Ontological Analyses and Ethical Implications* (New York: Galaxy Books, 1960), 18.

32. Ibid., 19.

33. Ibid., 19–21.

34. King, *A Comparison of the Conceptions of God*, 65.

35. Tillich, *Love, Power and Justice*, 35.

36. Ibid., 37.

37. King, *Where Do We Go from Here*, 37.

38. Ibid.

39. Tillich, *Love, Power, and Justice*, 40.

40. Ibid.

41. King, *Where Do We Go from Here*, 38–39 (emphasis added).

42. Ibid., 38.

4. Pastoral Caregiving as Shaped by King's Constructive Thought

1. Cone, *Black Theology of Liberation*, 50–53.

2. King, *Stride Toward Freedom*, 100.

3. See Walter E. Fluker, *They Looked for a City: A Comparative Analysis of the Ideal Community in the Thought of Howard Thurman and Martin Luther King, Jr.* (New York: University Press of America, 1989), 114.

4. Ibid. See also King, "Ethical Demands for Integration," 119.

5. King, "Ethical Demands for Integration," 119.

6. See Seward Hiltner, *Preface to Pastoral Theology* (Nashville: Abingdon, 1958), 89–172.

7. Edward P. Wimberly, *Pastoral Care in the Black Church* (Nashville: Abindgon, 1979), 19.

8. "Integration is creative, and is therefore more profound and far-reaching than desegration. Integration is the positive acceptance of desegration and the welcomed participation of Negroes into the total range of human activities. Integration is genuine intergroup, interpersonal doing. . . . Integration is the ultimate goal of our national community." King, "Ethical Demands for Integration," 118.

9. King, *Strength to Love*, 16.

10. For an excellent discussion of the concept of governing symbols, see William Johnson Everett, *God's Federal Republic: Reconstructing Our Governing Symbol* (New York: Paulist, 1988), 3–21.

11. See Howard Clinebell, *Basic Types of Pastoral Care and Counseling*, rev. ed. (Nashville: Abingdon, 1984), and *Contemporary Growth Therapies* (Nashville: Abingdon, 1981).

12. "Jesus took the phrase 'the Kingdom of God,' but he changed its meaning . . . Jesus made love the mark of sovereignty. . . . The Kingdom of God will be a society in which men and women live as children of God should live. It will be a kingdom controlled by the law of love . . . Many have attempted to say that the ideal of a better world will be worked out in the next world. But Jesus taught men to say, 'Thy will be done in earth, as it is in heaven.' Although the world seems to be in bad shape today, we must never lose faith in the power of God to achieve his purpose." King, "What a Christian Should Think About the Kingdom of God," King papers, special collections, Boston University, 2. Quoted in Kenneth L. Smith and Ira G. Zepp, *Search for the Beloved Community* (Valley Forge: Judson Press, 1974), 129.

13. John Stuart Mill, "Utilitarianism," in *Utilitarianism, On Liberty and Representative Government* (New York: E. P. Dutton, 1910), 6–11.

14. Ibid., 40–42.

15. Jeremiah 22:15–16: "Are you a king because you compete in cedar? Did not your father eat and drink and do justice and righteousness? Then it was well with him. He judged the cause of the poor and needy; then it was well. Is not this to know me? says the Lord."

16. James M. Efird, *The Old Testament Writings: History, Literature, and Interpretation* (Atlanta: John Knox Press, 1982), 160.

17. Hans W. Hertzberg, *Prophet und Gott* (Gutersloh: C. Berte Ismann, 1923), quoted by Jose Miranda in *Marx and the Bible: A Critique of the Philosophy of Oppression* (Maryknoll, N.Y.: Orbis, 1974), 127.

18. King, "Experiment in Love," in *A Testament of Hope*, 19.

19. Ibid.

20. Ibid., 20.

21. Ibid., 19.

5. The Practical Application of King's Thought

1. The proposals advanced in this chapter have been inspired and informed by the community psychology movement of the recent past. For a helpful discussion of this movement and its representative ideas, see Stanton L. Jones, "Community Psychology," in *Baker Encyclopedia of Psychology*, ed. David G. Benner (Grand Rapids: Baker Book House, 1985), 197–201; Jim Orford, *Community Psychology: Theory and Practice* (New York: John Wiley and Sons, 1992); Leonard D. Goodstein and Irwin Sandler, *American Psychologist* 33 (1978): 882–92; and George Albee, *American Psychologist* 37 (1982): 1043–50. I feel indebted to Jones in the cited article for the format of this presentation and some key ideas.

2. Fowler, *Faith Development and Pastoral Care*, 20–21.

3. For variant perspectives on how the vocation of pastoral care and counseling can embrace ecological concerns, see specifically Clinebell, *Contemporary Growth Therapies*, 193–94, 231–32, 270–71; "Looking Back, Looking Ahead," *Journal of Pastoral Care* 46, no. 3 (fall 1992): 263–72; and *Basic Types of Pastoral Care and Counseling*, 53.

4. Mbiti, *African Religions*, 141.

5. Fowler, *Faith Development and Pastoral Care,* 20–21.

6. Minuchin, *Families and Family Therapy* (Cambridge: Harvard University Press, 1974), 4–15.

7. Ibid.

8. "Constitution of the World Health Organization," in *Basic Documents,* 20th ed. (Geneva: World Health Organization, 1969), 1.

9. Ibid.

10. Ibid., 3.

11. See Brock Chisholm, "Mental Health and World Citizenship," in *International Congress and Mental Health,* vol. 4, *Proceedings of the International Conference on Mental Hygiene,* London, 1948, as quoted in Earl L. Sullivan, "The World Health Organization: A Functional Study of Politics and Health," Ph.D. dissertation, Claremont Graduate School, Claremont, Calif., 1969, 76. Sullivan reports that Brock Chisholm was chairman of the drafting committee of WHO's constitution.

12. WHO constitution, 2.

13. Nancy Boyd-Franklin, *Black Families in Therapy: A Multisystems Approach* (New York: Guilford Press, 1989).

14. August B. Hollingshead and Frederick C. Redlich, "Social Stratification and Psychiatric Disorders," *American Sociological Review* 18 (1953): 167. See also William C. Cockerham, *Sociology of Mental Disorder,* 3d ed. (Englewood Cliffs, N.J.: Prentice Hall, 1992), 151–56. The designations of upper-class, upper-middle-class, lower-middle-class, working-class, and lower-class to correspond with the researchers' I, II, III, IV, and V classifications were proposed by Cockerham.

15. Hollingshead and Redlich, "Social Stratification," 167.

16. Ibid.

17. Ibid., 168.

18. Leo Levy and Louis Rowitz, *The Ecology of Mental Disorder* (New York: Behavioral Publications, 1973), 39–62.

19. Marilyn J. Rosenstein, Henry J. Steadman, Laura J. Milazzo-Sayre, Robin L. MacAskill, and Ronald W. Manderscheid, *Characteristics of Admissions to the Inpatient Services of State and County Mental Hospitals, United States, 1980,* Mental Health Statistical Note, 177 (Rockville, Md.: U.S. Dept. of Health and Human Services, 1986).

20. Marilyn Rosenstein, Henry Steadman, and Laura Milazzo-Sayre, *Characteristics of Admissions to Private Psychiatric Hospital Inpatient Services, United States, 1980,* Mental Health Statistical Note, 174 (Rockville, Md.: U.S. Dept. of Health and Human Services, 1986). See also Cockerham, *Sociology of Mental Disorder,* 169.

21. Rosenstein et al., *Characteristics of Admissions to Private Psychiatric Hospital Inpatient Services,* 174.

22. See S. Seymour Kety and Steven Matthysse, "Genetic and Biochemical Aspects of Schizophrenia," in *The New Harvard Guide to Psychiatry,* ed. Armand M. Nicholi Jr. (Cambridge: Belknap Press of Harvard University Press, 1988), 139–51; and Gerald C. Davison and John M. Neale, *Abnormal Psychology,* 2d ed. (New York: John Wiley and Sons, 1986), 333–59.

23. Davison and Neale, *Abnormal Psychology,* 346.

24. Ibid.
25. Orford, *Community Psychology,* 46.
26. Davison and Neale, *Abnormal Psychology,* 348.
27. Kety and Matthysse, *New Harvard Guide,* 281.
28. Orford, *Community Psychology,* 101.
29. Ibid., 101–02.
30. U.S. Bureau of the Census, *Statistical Abstract of the United States 1992,* 112th ed. (Washington, D.C.: GPO, 1992), 85.
31. Ibid.
32. Ibid. The following are suicide rates for various age groups: Males ages 45–54 (22.4), ages 55–64 (24.6), ages 65–74 (33.0), ages 75–84 (51.3) and 85 years and over (66.7). Females ages 45–54 (7.3), ages 55–64 (7.3), ages 65–74 (5.9), ages 75–84 (6.0), and 85 years and over (5.8).
33. Ibid.
34. Ibid.
35. Ibid., 90.
36. Alec Roy, ed., *Suicide* (Baltimore: Williams and Wilkins, 1986), 2. See also Cockerham, *Sociology of Mental Disorder,* 104–08; and Edwin S. Shneidman, "Some Essentials of Suicide and Some Implications for Response," in *Suicide,* ed. Alec Roy, 1.
37. Cockerham, *Sociology of Mental Disorder,* 105.
38. Shneidman, "Some Essentials of Suicide," 3. The author refers to an unpublished joint questionnaire by the American Medical Association and the American Psychiatric Association as the source of this classification.
39. Morton Kramer, Earl S. Pollack, Richard W. Redick, and Ben Z. Locke, *Mental Disorders/Suicide* (Cambridge: Harvard University Press, 1972), 174.
40. Shneidman, "Some Essentials of Suicide," 4–12.
41. See Keith Hawton, "Suicide in Adolescents," in *Suicide,* 135–50.
42. See Peter Sainsbury, "The Epidemiology of Suicide," in *Suicide,* 17–45.

Afterword

1. Jones, "Community Psychology," 199.
2. Ibid.
3. Ibid., 199–200.
4. Ibid., 200.
5. Ibid.

SELECTED BIBLIOGRAPHY

Adler, Alfred. "Early Recollections and Dreams." In *The Individual Psychology of Alfred Adler: A Systematic Presentation in Selections from His Writings,* edited by Heinz L. Ansbacher and Rowena R. Ansbacher. New York: Basic Books, 1956.

Bell, Derrick. *Civil Rights: Leading Cases.* Boston: Little, Brown and Co., 1980.

Beryman, Jerome, ed. *Life Maps: Conversations on the Journey of Faith: Jim Fowler and Sam Keen.* Waco, Tex.: Word, 1978.

Boyd-Franklin, Nancy. *Black Families in Therapy: A Multisystems Approach.* New York: Guilford Press, 1989.

Calvin, John. *Commentaries on the First Book of Moses Called Genesis.* Vol. 1. Translated by John King. Grand Rapids: Eerdmans, 1948.

Chittister, Joan. *Job's Daughters: Women and Power.* New York: Paulist Press, 1990.

Clinebell, Howard. *Contemporary Growth Therapies: Resources for Actualizing Human Wholeness.* Nashville: Abingdon, 1981.

————. *Basic Types of Pastoral Care and Counseling: Resources for the Ministry of Health and Growth.* Rev. ed. Nashville: Abingdon, 1984.

Cockerham, William C. *Sociology of Mental Disorder.* 3d ed. Englewood Cliffs, N.J.: Prentice Hall, 1992.

Cone, James H. *Black Theology of Liberation.* Philadelphia: J. B. Lippincott, 1970.

Daly, Mary. *Beyond God the Father.* Boston: Beacon Press, 1985.

Davidson, Basil. *The African Slave Trade.* Boston: Little, Brown and Co., 1980.

Davison, Gerald C., and John M. Neale. *Abnormal Psychology.* 2d ed. New York: John Wiley and Sons, 1986.

Efird, James M. *The Old Testament Writings: History, Literature, and Interpretation.* Atlanta: John Knox Press, 1982.

Enns, Paul. *The Moody Handbook of Theology.* Chicago: Moody Press, 1989.

Erik H. Erikson, *Childhood and Society.* 2d ed. New York: W. W. Norton, 1963.

————. *Dimensions of a New Identity.* New York: W. W. Norton, 1974.

————. *Identity and the Life Cycle.* New York: W. W. Norton, 1980.

————. *Identity, Youth and Crisis.* New York: W. W. Norton, 1968.

Everett, William Johnson. *God's Federal Republic: Reconstructing Our Governing Symbol.* New York: Paulist Press, 1988.

Fluker, Walter E. *They Looked for a City: A Comparative Analysis of the Ideal Community in the Thought of Howard Thurman and Martin Luther King, Jr.* New York: University Press of America, 1989.

Fowler, James W. *Becoming Adult, Becoming Christian: Adult Development and Christian Faith.* San Francisco: Harper and Row, 1984.

————. *Faith Development and Pastoral Care.* Philadelphia: Fortress Press, 1987.

————. *Stages of Faith: The Psychology of Human Development and the Quest for Meaning.* San Francisco: Harper and Row, 1981.

Fowler, James W. and Robin W. Lovin, eds. *Trajectories in Faith.* Nashville: Abingdon Press, 1980.

Frazier, E. Franklin *The Negro Church in America.* New York: Schocken Books, 1974.

Gilligan, Carol. *In a Different Voice: Psychological Theory and Women's Development.* Cambridge: Harvard University Press, 1982.

Gossett, Thomas F. *Race: The History of an Idea in America.* Dallas: Southern Methodist University Press, 1963.

Grant, Jacquelyn. *White Women's Christ and Black Women's Jesus: Feminist Christology and Womanist Response.* Atlanta: Scholars Press, 1989.

Haller, John S., Jr. *Outcasts from Evolution: Scientific Attitudes of Racial Inferiority, 1859–1900.* Urbana: University of Illinois Press, 1971.

Hiltner, Seward. *Preface to Pastoral Theology.* Nashville: Abingdon, 1958.

Ho, Man Keung, *Family Therapy with Ethnic Minorities.* Beverly Hills, Calif.: Sage Publications, 1987.

Kegan, Robert. *The Evolving Self: Problem and Process in Human Development.* Cambridge: Harvard University Press, 1982.

King, Martin Luther, Jr. "Chronology." In *The Words of Martin Luther King, Jr.: Selected by Coretta Scott King.* New York: Newmarket Press, 1983.

———. *A Comparison of the Conceptions of God in the Thinking of Paul Tillich and Henry Nelson Wieman.,* Ph.D. dissertation, Boston University, 1955. Ann Arbor: UMI, 1977.

———. *Strength to Love.* New York: Harper and Row, 1963.

———. *Stride Toward Freedom: The Montgomery Story.* New York: Harper and Row, 1958.

———. *A Testament of Hope: The Essential Writings of Martin Luther King, Jr.* Edited by James M. Washington. San Francisco: Harper and Row, 1986.

———. *The Trumpet of Conscience.* New York: Harper and Row, 1968.

———. *Where Do We Go From Here: Chaos or Community?* New York: Harper and Row, 1967.

———. *Why We Can't Wait.* New York: Harper and Row, 1963.

Kramer, Morton, et al. *Mental Disorders/Suicide.* Cambridge: Harvard University Press, 1972.

Lerner, Gerda. *The Creation of Patriarchy.* New York: Oxford University Press, 1986.

Levy, Leo, and Louis Rowitz. *The Ecology of Mental Disorder.* New York: Behavioral Publications, 1973.

Lincoln, C. Eric. *The Black Church Since Frazier.* New York: Schocken Books, 1974

McGoldrick, Monica, et al. eds. *Ethnicity and Family Therapy.* New York: Guilford Press, 1982.

Maddi, Salvatore R. *Personality Theories: A Comparative Analysis.* 4th ed. Homewood, Ill.: Dorsey Press, 1980.

Mbiti, John S. *African Religions and Philosophy.* Garden City, N.Y.: Doubleday, 1970.

Mill, John Stuart. "Utilitarianism." In *Utilitarianism, On Liberty and Representative Government.* New York: E. P. Dutton, 1910.

Miranda, Jose. *Marx and the Bible: A Critique of the Philosophy of Oppression.* Maryknoll, N.Y.: Orbis, 1974.

Orford, Jim. *Community Psychology: Theory and Practice.* New York: John Wiley and Sons, 1992.

Quarles, Benjamin. *The Negro in the Making of America.* New York: Macmillan, 1964.

Report of the National Advisory Commission on Civil Disorders. New York: Bantam Books, 1968.

Rodney, Walter. *How Europe Underdeveloped Africa.* Washington, D.C.: Howard University Press, 1974.

Rosenstein, Marilyn, Henry Steadman, and Laura Milazzo-Sayre. *Characteristics of Admissions to Private Psychiatric Hospital Inpatient Services, United States, 1980.* Mental Health Statistical Note, 174. Rockville, Md.: U.S. Dept. of Health and Human Services, 1986.

Rosenstein, Marilyn J., et al. *Characteristics of Admissions to the Inpatient Services of State and County Mental Hospitals, United States, 1980.* Mental Health Statistical Note, 177 Rockville, Md.: U.S. Dept. of Health and Human Services, 1986.

Roy, Alec, ed., *Suicide.* Baltimore: Williams and Wilkins, 1986.

Ruether, Rosemary Radford. *Sexism and God-Talk: Toward a Feminist Theology.* Boston: Beacon Press, 1983.

Sainsbury, Peter. "The Epidemiology of Suicide." In *Suicide.* Edited by Alec Roy. Baltimore: Williams and Wilkins, 1986.

Sanford, Linda Tschirhart, and Mary Ellen Donovan. *Women and Self-Esteem.* New York: Penguin Books, 1984.

Smith, Kenneth L., and Ira G. Zepp. *Search for the Beloved Community.* Valley Forge, Pa.: Judson Press, 1974.

Three Negro Classics: Up From Slavery, Booker T. Washington; The Souls of Black Folk, William E. B. DuBois; The Autobiography of an Ex-Colored Man, James Weldon Johnson. New York: Avon Books, 1965.

Tillich, Paul. *The Courage to Be.* New Haven: Yale University Press, 1980.

————. *Love, Power and Justice: Ontological Analyses and Ethical Implications.* New York: Galaxy Books, 1960.

Tucker, Cynthia. "Behind Bars." Atlanta Journal/Atlanta Constitution 17 (January 1993).

U.S. Dept. of Labor, Bureau of Labor Statistics. Employment and Earnings 38, no. 12 (December 1991) Washington, D.C.: GPO, 1991.

U.S. Bureau of the Census, Current Population Reports. *Poverty in the United States: 1990.* Series P-60, no. 175. Washington, D.C.: GPO, 1991.

U.S. Bureau of the Census. *Statistical Abstract of the United States: 1991.* 111th ed. Washington, D.C.: GPO, 1991.

U.S. Bureau of the Census, *Statistical Abstract of the United States 1992.* 112th ed. Washington, D.C.: GPO, 1992.

United Nations. *The World's Women 1970–1990: Trends and Statistics.* Social Statistics and Indicators, Series K, no. 8. New York: UN, 1991.

Westkutt, Marcia. *The Feminist Legacy of Karen Horney.* New Haven: Yale University Press, 1986.

Wimberly, Edward P. *Pastoral Care in the Black Church.* Nashville: Abingdon Press, 1979.

Witvliet, Theo. *A Place in the Sun: An Introduction to Liberation Theology in the Third World.* Maryknoll, N.Y.: Orbis Books, 1985.

Woodson, Carter G., *The Mis-Education of the Negro* (1933) Reprint, Washington, D.C.: Associated Publishers, 1972.

INDEX

oppression: anatomy and patterns of,
1–28; defined, xx–xxi, 1–2; economic, 4,
8, 71–72, 82–84; and educational
opportunity, 5–6, 8; and identity
formation, 13–22; and Jesus, 46–47;
and powerlessness, 43–53; realization
of, 43–44; and self-esteem, 25–28,
43–53; of women, 2–6. *See also* racial
oppression
Orford, Jim, 94, 96
original sin, 2–3
Original Sin of Being Born Female, 15
origin of species, 3

pacific peace, 61, 62
Parks, Rosa, xv
Parks, Sharon, 90
participation, 63; political, 4, 9
pastoral caregiving, xvi–xx, 54–66;
anthropological norm, 54–56; community model, 67–78, 81–84; compared
with pastoral counseling, xviii–xix; conciliation task, 57; ecological dimension,
67, 71–78; evocation symbol of, 59–66;
hyperindividualistic model, 56, 60;
King's contributions to, 79–84; psychological norm, 54–56; public policy
dimension, 67, 78; reclamation task,
56–57; theological norm, 54–56; transcendence task, 58–59; transformation
task, 57–58; vocation of, xvii, xx–xxi
patients, xviii
patyagraha, 65–66
Paul, 7
Pauline-Lutheran doctrine of justification
by faith, 21
peace metaphor, 60–62, 70–71
Pearce, John K., 89
Pedagogy of the Oppressed (Freire), 22
penis envy, 3, 14
periphery of personality, 13, 16
personality: core of, 13, 16; development
of, 13; development of, in females,
14–16; epistemological attribute of,
13–14, 16; ontological attribute of,

13–14, 16, 55; periphery of, 13, 16.
See also identity
Piaget, Jean, 35
Pityana, Nyameko, 89, 90
Place in the Sun, A (Witvliet), 17
Plessy v. Ferguson (1896), 9
political participation, 4, 9
Pollack, Earl S., 96
population density, 1
poverty, 8, 12, 71–72, 82–84
power: in ecological pastoral caregiving,
74–78; nature of, 51–53; ontological
view of, 52–53; power differentials,
27–28; purposes of, 51–53
Power, F. Clark, 88
powerlessness, 27–28; defined, xxi; in
ecological pastoral caregiving, 74–78;
and identity, 43–53; King on, 50–51;
and self-esteem, 50–51
praxis, defined, xxi
prescription, 23
priesthood, for women, 4–5
prison populations, 11
processive peace, 61
psychoanalytic movement, xvii–xviii
psychological power, 27
psychotherapy: hyperindividualistic
model, xvii–xix; intrapsychic orientation
to, xvii, 31; psychoanalytic orientation,
xvii–xviii
psychotic disorders, 71–72
public policy, 67, 78
Pygmies, 1

Quarles, Benjamin, 86

racial groups, 6–7, 13, 46
racial oppression, 6–8; and civil rights,
8–9; and ecclesiastical leadership, 9–10;
and economic oppression, 8; and educational opportunity, 8, 10–11; and identity, 16–22; and incarceration rates, 11;
and political participation, 9; and
poverty, 12; psychological theories of, 7;
scientific theories of, 7; and segregation